Four Girls from Berlin

Der Alte Fritz and Lotte

Four Girls from Berlin

A True Story of a Friendship That Defied the Holocaust

Marianne Meyerhoff

John Wiley & Sons, Inc.

Published by John Wiley & Sons, Inc., Hoboken, New Jersey
Published simultaneously in Canada

Wiley Bicentennial Logo: Richard J. Pacifico

All photographs courtesy of Corky McCoy except those on pages 174 and 193, which are courtesy of the United States Holocaust Museum, Washington, D.C.

For general information about our other products and services, please contact our Customer Care Department within the United States at (800) 762-2974, outside the United States at (317) 572-3993 or fax (317) 572-4002.

Wiley also publishes its books in a variety of electronic formats. Some content that appears in print may not be available in electronic books. For more information about Wiley products, visit our web site at www.wiley.com.

Library of Congress Cataloging-in-Publication Data

Meyerhoff, Marianne.
    Four girls from Berlin : a true story of a friendship that defied the Holocaust / Marianne Meyerhoff.
        p. cm.
    ISBN 978-0-471-22405-1 (cloth : alk. paper)
    ISBN 978-1-68442-590-7 (paperback)
    1. Jews—California—Los Angeles—Biography. 2. Jews, German—California—Los Angeles—Biography. 3. Refugees, Jewish—California—Los Angeles—Biography. 4. Children of Holocaust survivors—California—Los Angeles—Biography. 5. Mothers and daughters—California—Los Angeles—Biography. 6. Los Angeles (Calif.)—Biography. I. Title.
    F869.L89 J5545 2007
    940.53'180922—dc22
    [B]
                                                                            2007006192

Printed in the United States of America

For Joel, who helped me find my voice

Time was running out when my grandfather took a sheet of paper and typed out the names of his family and friends. He did not want them to be forgotten. Later, perhaps when he no longer had the use of a typewriter, he added other names in pencil. The vast emptiness of the rest of the page speaks poignantly to me of children and children's children never born who would have populated my world. I dedicate this book to the memory of them all.

Familien

Timendorfer,
Wachsner,
Spitzer
und deren Freunde.

Schlesinger, Pese
Rosenbund, Goldstein
Müller Gerstel
Bergmann

Wolff Apoland

CONTENTS

ACKNOWLEDGMENTS

Rena Namgalies was the first to plant the seed in my mind to set the story of my mother and her girlfriends to paper. Lady Elizabeth Longford said I must do it. She said the world needed its heroines, and she never let me forget.

Years later, I interviewed Holocaust survivor Paula Lindemann for the Shoah Foundation. She was familiar with a form of German script used in the early twentieth century and offered to translate and bring back to life a cache of old family documents of mine, most of which, until then, had remained a mystery. Some of them appear in this book.

Sarah Ogilvie and Scott Miller of the U.S. Holocaust Museum in Washington, D.C., marveled that this cache of documents presented a rare window on Jewish family life in nineteeth- and twentieth-century Germany. They set me on a course that led me to Hana Lane, senior editor at John Wiley & Sons, whose wise counsel, along with the copyediting prowess of her colleague, senior production editor Lisa Burstiner, have added immeasurably to the final draft of this book.

Maurice Herz, linguist extraordinaire, went through the manuscript with a fine-tooth comb, and Corky McCoy's fine eye and photographic skills have been most helpful.

Ari Zev of the USC Shoah Foundation for Visual History and Education went out of his way from the very beginning to help me at every turn.

I also owe a world of gratitude to Jack Cummings, Barry Dennen, Phylis Dubow, J. Fishman, Allan Goldstein, Mikael Kehler, Connie La Maida, and Eva Silver for their unswerving concern and encouragement, and to my stepdaughter, Jill Steinberger, for her keen insights.

For their emotional, technical, and practical support, I offer them all my heartfelt appreciation.

PROLOGUE

My world dawns upon the eyes of my mother. She picks me up and holds me in her arms, and she peers searchingly, dreamingly into my eyes. I will always remember her eyes through the eyes of a three-year-old. They radiate overwhelming love and need in a blend of perpetual surprise, as if I am a miracle.

"*Was suchst du wenn du mir so tief in die Augen schaust, Mutti*? What is it you look for in my eyes so deeply, so urgently, Mommy?"

My mother, Charlotte Wachsner Meyerhoff, set me down on the side of my cot, which was covered with a khaki army surplus blanket. To this day, I hate the feel of coarse wool against my skin. I still hear the scrape of the wooden chair as she pulled it close to me across the cold cement floor of the garage that was our home in Los Angeles. Her native language was German, and she was fluent in Latin and French but not in English. For some reason she resisted it, though she struggled hard to learn it.

I loved a Mexican song everyone was singing in 1944, so Mutti listened to it on the radio and learned the Spanish lyrics by heart just so she could sing them to me. She sat next to me with her magnificent lute, the antique one that her father, the professor, had given her for her tenth birthday, and sang to me in Spanish.

"*Für Ma-ri-an-na*," she said, pronouncing my name the European way, "*für meine schöne Mädchen*, for my beautiful little girl." It was my own

I

private concert. Mutti did not understand the lyrics to "Cielito Lindo" or the irony of how fitting they were for us.

"*Canta y no llores. Porque cantando se alegran, cielito lindo, los corazones.* Sing and do not cry. For by singing, hearts become gay."

Her voice gave me joy, and my joy was all she lived for, so she added "Cielito Lindo" to the permanent repertoire of her favorite songs she loved to sing, the great music of Beethoven and Mendelssohn and Brahms and Schubert and Richard Strauss, and the racy cabaret tunes of Kurt Weil and Bertolt Brecht from exciting, cosmopolitan Berlin, where she was born and had come of age.

All I need to do is close my eyes to call upon that long-ago moment, as I have over the years, and see it again in sharp detail, like a waking dream. My sad Mutti sings, and she, too, is transfigured with joy. Her eyes, now mirthful, dart everywhere like a diva granting encores to the worshipful audience that but for Hitler would have been hers. Her voice floats like a velvet caress that lingers in the mind. In her rapture, she would have me sail with her on a great voyage to a magic place called happiness. But when her song ends, so ends her rapture. The vestige of a smile lingers on her face but is only a veneer. It cannot mask from me her torment that lies just beneath. I am not yet four years old, but I know that I am the stronger. I reach out to touch her face, and her eyes infuse me with her trauma. With the certainty of the child I reassure her, "*Macht dir keine Sorgen, Mutti.* Please don't worry, Mommy. You will not be disappointed. All that you look for in my eyes you are sure to find in me." I am mother to my mother. I am all she has in the world to console her.

CHAPTER I

Glimpses of a Shattered Past

I WAS A COLLECTOR OF VIGNETTES from my mother's life, out-of-sequence fragments revealed in a hush in unguarded moments. Sometimes in the night she cried out for her father in her sleep, "Papi!" Or was it I who cried out in my own dreams for mine?

Her lips trembled, "Mops, Mops."

Who is Mops? In time, I wrested from her that Mops was the pet name she had given to her younger brother, my Uncle Ernst, who exulted, as did my whole family in Berlin, when the news reached them from America that I had been born. My mother was five years old when Mops came into the world. At the very mention of his name she could barely contain her remorse. Mutti was not willing, in her waking consciousness, to talk of him, although thoughts of Mops were never far from her mind. Sometimes, when I displayed a certain characteristic or made her laugh by doing mischief, she let slip, "You come by your impishness honestly. Your Uncle Ernst used to do that. You remind me so much of him."

When she watched a comedian, she lost herself in laughter, but while she laughed, she was sad. So was I sad. Isn't that the way it always is, the natural condition? Isn't everybody sad, and how is a child to know the difference if she is born into it? Mutti was then just as innocent, as new to America, as I was to the world. I was her world. She knew little English, knew not a soul, and had no money. She didn't want to talk about "what happened."

As the years passed, I invented two techniques that might encourage her to talk. The first one was to take a chance and brave it out, constantly pestering her to answer my question. Then, just to find peace, she might yield to what I asked and, having done so, talk a little more. The second way was to become completely silent when Mutti would not answer a question, with the hope that she might, on her own, feel compelled to fill the void. When she did answer questions that I asked, she spoke with an economy of words. I felt guilty then, for pushing her. I feel guilty now as I remember, because the recounting of such things caused her to relive them with unabated pain.

Perhaps Mutti was not reliving the pain. Maybe that was where she spent most of her time, emerging into the present only out of necessity to perform her motherly duties. She might have been visiting Mops or replaying a time with her father, Herr Professor Doktor Fritz Wachsner, or her stepmother, Paula, the only mother she'd ever known, or the three grandmothers she adored, or her courtly uncle Heinrich, or all the rest of her uncles and aunts and cousins and the extended family she had left behind in Germany. She never conquered the despair of no longer having them in her life. I still see her eyelids flutter on her pillow as she recaptured a moment with them in the timeless imagery of the mind.

It remained for a child to intuit what Mutti saw in her dreams. Intuition was the mortar that held together the few building stones, the contradictions and meager facts I knew of my lost family. In the waking state, the disconnected memories she let slip told no narrative—they were just shards of a broken mirror that still held shattered glimpses of her former life. To talk freely of this might open the floodgates too wide and sweep away the precious little she clung to of her hidden, vanished world. Today, when she is no longer here, endless unformed questions still float just beyond the edge of my consciousness. No matter how much I come to know, I rue the gaps

4

I will never fill that lead me to conjecture. Making sense of it all is an ever-evolving pastiche for me to sort out if I would understand my own story.

Mutti wanted me to think that the time before I was born did not exist, that life began for her when she came to America. No less is true for other refugees. But if her physical being was now safe, she had left much of her mind, heart, and soul in Germany. And although I was born in America, as much a part of me was there with her in Germany. As years passed, Mutti chose to exhume more, even initiating conversations by opening herself to tormenting recall, "so their faces will not be erased as if they never lived at all, as if what happened to them didn't matter."

From the time I learned to talk, Mutti spoke to me as if I were an adult, the better not to love me as a child. All we had was each other, and I knew she loved me with her whole being, as I loved her. But she was cautious with her affection and rarely kissed me. What is a childhood without kisses? She would not let herself feel too much in case that which was dear might once again be taken from her. This was her barren world in which I grew to consciousness.

She invited me to call her by her first name.

"You may call me Lotte."

"I just want to call you Mommy."

She picked me up. She did not hug me to her. She held me at arm's length. The warmth I got from her came from her eyes. "Then call me Mutti, too."

It struck other children as odd to hear me call her by her first name. I never heard them address their mothers this way.

"But we are friends, as well," she added, her inflection suggesting that friendship was the higher virtue. The recollection still stings with rejection.

When I was old enough to read and write, she gave me a journal.

"Do you have a journal, Lotte?" I asked.

"No more."

"But why?"

"It is ended."

5

To what level of hopelessness must a person sink to say her story is ended?

"I threw my journal in the sea. I almost threw myself overboard with it. Thank God, I did not, for then I would not have had you. I do not wish to talk of things you do not need to hear. It is better, perhaps, when you are older."

"I do need to hear."

"*Bitte*, please, then you be the one to keep a journal. You be the one to remember."

From then on, I kept a journal, and for a time, while I grew up, it was my only friend and confidante.

Somewhere along the way, I ferreted out of Mutti that my father had left Germany and sailed to Cuba on the day of their marriage, December 16, 1938. Mutti followed him six months later aboard the Hamburg Amerika liner the SS *St. Louis*, a nightmare voyage that she refused to talk about for years. Not until I was older did I learn that the *St. Louis* had been forced to sail back to Europe, where my mother was interred in Westerbork Detention Camp. Then I heard the story of how she escaped the clutches of Hitler by the narrowest of margins.

With no money for rent, we moved from room to room until Mutti found a garage for us to live in. It was in Watts in South Central Los Angeles, which then, as now, was mainly a black neighborhood. The garage was the first home I remember. It had a cold water tap and a basin for all our washing needs.

The day we moved in, we were on a crowded bus on the way to our new home. In our arms, on our laps, and spilling into the aisle were paper bags holding everything we owned. For Mutti's eighteenth birthday, her father, the professor, had gotten her a wonderful heavy greatcoat for the bitter Berlin winters. The coat was old and worn now, but the gift from her father was something he had touched and thus was an extension of him, gone from this earth. She was not yet ready to give up either. Who wears such a coat on a mild spring day in Los Angeles? Mutti did, to avoid carrying one extra thing when her hands were full. The American modes and styles she had lived in the midst of for nearly four years, since immigrating, had no influence on her. Nor did American women wear their hair the way she did: long braids pulled back tight and rolled up in a severe bun. I stuck out, too, like a Raggedy Ann with my mop of curly red hair. Passengers stared, even more so when Mutti widened the gulf by talking in German to me. The one I loved embarrassed me. Strangers' eyes seemed unwelcoming as they burned into us. We didn't belong.

We awoke in the garage the next morning to the sound of children laughing and playing and mothers chatting outside on the street. Mutti bathed me with cold water in the laundry tub, then dressed me and told me to go outside and play.

"The voices of children that now you hear playing belong to new friends that you soon will be making," she intoned in her sing-song, lyrical Berlin German.

I was just beginning to learn halting English and was too shy to go out by myself to play. She would have to take me. Mutti had her own aversion to meeting new people. Self-effacing in her new country, she was quick to spurn any attention that came her way. But she had been raised to strict German discipline and so when impelled knew how to deal with her social anxieties. Those she held inside were not so readily conquered.

Resolute, she took me by the hand and marched me out to the street. On the lawns and the sidewalks, mothers with coffee cups and cigarettes turned and looked our way. Children stopped playing and stared. Through our hands, clenched together firm as an umbilical cord, I felt her tremble. Her fear legitimized my own. An eon passed before a mother, whom we soon learned was our next-door neighbor, unthawed the tableau with a "Good morning" and a smile. Mutti managed to send back a smile of her own. For weeks afterward, I went outside to play but stood on the sidewalk instead and watched other children play. They belonged.

What is family? I had neither concept nor sense of family. There were no photographs to connect me to the past but one, a picture of my father, Warren Meyerhoff, who had joined the army and was now a U.S. infantry sergeant fighting somewhere in Europe. I had still been an infant when Daddy enlisted. I didn't remember him, but I idolized his picture and longed for him with all my being.

"Just like you," Mutti said, "I was a little girl waiting for my father to come home from war."

"Do you mean there was a different war when you were little, Mutti?"

She nodded her head sadly. "A very different war. *Siehst du, meine süsse*, you see, my sweet little one, Jews fought then for Deutschland alongside their fellow Germans. *Ja*, it was a very different war."

And now, my father, my hero, had gone back to Europe to fight and protect us from a great German evil. I did not understand.

"*Sind wir auch nicht Deutsch?* Are we not Germans, too?"

"*Ja*," Mutti answered, unmindful of her residual pride, "we are Germans. But, *meine Tochter*, my daughter, you were born in America and are first an American."

"But if my father is German, why is he fighting other Germans?"

Heartsick for her Deutschland, Mutti groped for an answer that I might understand while her eyes flooded for the beloved homeland that had cast her out. Her tears of rejection were contagious, for I wept, too, and felt the victim of whom or of what I did not know or understand and, for that, was all the more terrified. The mantle of victim is poison to the psyche. Lifelong pondering of the dark side is no antidote, for who could ever come to a whole understanding of evil in such awesome dimensions? But I will never forget the simple answer that Mutti gave to my question that day.

"Most people are good. There are some who are not. No less is true in Deutschland. But, in this world, *Liebchen*, there are few among us who are at all times the one or the other. *Mehr als das gibst uns nicht zu wissen.* More than this we are not given to know." She took my father's picture and *kusst* her "good German." I kissed him, too.

"He will return soon. A day is coming in *die Zukunft*, the future, when we will be together and safe in America forever." Nothing brought more happiness than imagining that day. We would have a hero to take care of us. He would know how to make us not be afraid in the night.

We were walking down a street one day and passed a five-and-dime. In the window were children's birthday supplies and party favors, little crepe paper–covered tubes that opened with a pop when pulled at the ends to reveal a surprise inside. I had to have one and nagged and pleaded with Mutti. Every cent meant a lot in those days, but she took me inside and bought it for me. Outside on the street, I pulled on the ends of the tube, and, with a pop, a little cross fell out on the sidewalk. I felt an instant, powerful fascination and bent down to pick it up.

"No, you cannot have that," Mutti said.

"But why?"

"Because we are Jews."

Just the same, she took me to the Unitarian church for my religious education to hear the inspirational sermons of the Reverend Stephen Fritchman, whose words I carry in my heart to this day. But what of the transcendental beauty of Judaism and the meaning of being Jewish? Of these, she told me little. Even as a child, I knew some precious thing had been smashed that I had to make whole again, realizing all the while that it could never be put back together as it was.

Mutti told me to pick up the little cross and put it on the bench at the bus stop, "so a little Christian child might find it and give it the love it deserves."

I remember the incident of the little cross because Mutti linked it immediately to a name, as we continued on down the street, a name that came floating up from the deepest recess of her mind as a gift once uttered never to be buried again.

"Rabbiner Gottschalk. I wonder what happened to dear Rabbiner Gottschalk. Reverend Dr. Benno Gottschalk."

"Who is he?"

"A rabbi I once knew. My father's best friend. Rabbiner of the New Reform Synagogue of Berlin at Johannesstrasse 15. He came every Friday night for Sabbath dinner."

"Tell me about him, Lotte."

"He was a towering presence, charming, and rugged as a movie star. I had a crush on him when I was hardly older than you. I was not alone.

He was the only rabbi my girlfriends ever met. They were taken with him, too. Everybody was. His home was beautiful. He gave me the first book I ever owned, a book of his essays. Everyone in Berlin was reading his book those days. He was like an uncle to me." With a wrinkled brow she shook her head sadly. "I wonder," she kept repeating to herself, "I wonder what happened to him, dear Rabbiner Gottschalk."

Our street in Watts was just around the corner from what is known today as the Watts Towers. On my first day of kindergarten, Mutti held my hand as we crossed the street. We turned a corner and there was Simon Rodia, bending and lifting as always, hard at work erecting out of his fantasy and broken bits of colored glass and pottery his magical towers that one day would be a landmark, his great legacy to the city of Los Angeles.

"*Gut Morgen, Frau Meyerhoff*," he shouted.

"*Nein*, it is '*Guten Morgen*,' Signore Rodia. *Buon giorno*," she called back, waving as she corrected his German and returned the courtesy in his native tongue.

I loved to climb and swing on the colorful towers.

"*Nein, meine kleine Afe*," she said to me, waving a finger. "Not today, my little monkey. Here, there will be no swinging this morning."

She was taking me to school, on my first day. Or was I taking her? For soon Mutti was lost. She hadn't the English or the confidence to approach passersby, so it was I who had to ask for directions.

At school, I became wholly immersed for the first time in the English language with no German to fall back on. I felt overwhelmed by a chasm of separation, for I had to say good-bye to Mutti and stay with the children. My frightened classmates felt abandoned by their mothers, and they cried for them. I cried, too, but it was I who had abandoned my mother, and I worried whether she would be able to manage, for she had never in her life, since the time of my birth, spent a moment alone without me.

In kindergarten I met a little blue-eyed girl with blond hair, and soon we were best friends. How I admired and envied her. All real American girls had blue eyes and blond hair. We became inseparable.

I was elated to belong somewhere aside from my relationship with my mother. I could not wait to go to school every day.

One day, I went around the corner to her house. We were playing in front when her grandfather came out in a huff, angrily stabbing his finger at me.

"You started the war," he hissed. "We don't want any Germans around here. Go home, you little Jewgirl."

He pulled his granddaughter inside and slammed the door in my face.

Was there something wrong with me? Who was I? Jew, Unitarian, German, American? The familiar shame of the outcast came over me. How distorted, when it was he who should have been ashamed. Terror clutched me then as it clutches me now when I return to that time: the racing of my heart, feeling belittled and not as good as, always the outsider.

The next day in the schoolyard my "best" friend called me a "little Jewgirl." I pulled her hair and threw her down. Other children backed away from me as if I were a pariah. I did not want to cry in front of them. The teacher witnessed all of this, but it was me she ordered to "Go sit in the corner." I never could tell Mutti. My instincts said it would remand her back to a terror beyond comprehension. And still I envied the little girl because her grandpa, bigot though he was, came and fetched her every day after school.

"If only I had a grandpa, how much I would love him. Where is my grandpa?" Too late, I felt my question break Mutti's heart. Her silence lay bare the answer. Sorrow pulsated with every beat of my own heart. She was too proud a woman to be pitied. I would have held her if only she'd have let me, but she would not. I couldn't comprehend why my love was not enough to fill her emptiness. I was left to drift in my own feelings of inadequacy and loss and sadness.

I heard the children talking in the street about fireworks. They said a holiday they called the Fourth of July was coming in the summer. But before it came, something unimaginable happened that dwarfed all else. Just before my fourth birthday, on May 20, 1945,

Adolf Hitler killed himself. A few days later, Germany surrendered unconditionally, and the war in Europe was over. I remember the whole neighborhood milling in the street. Mutti picked me up and danced me around the garage. She was staring oddly that way, peering into my eyes as if she couldn't believe we were out of harm's way, searching them for some hidden meaning as if I were a miracle and an oracle rolled into one. I saw a confusing mix of terror and relief in her eyes. With my eyes of today, I understand better what I saw: how odd that Hitler is dead and we Jews are still alive.

Before we knew their fate, our hearts were filled with tears for our brethren, Jews and every other victim. But now that Allied victory had brought the war to a close, the disaster overcame and engulfed us and spun us even deeper into its eddy. Mutti was frightened, more so than ever, for soon she would face learning the fate of her loved ones. Yet even worse would be not learning their fate. Once a victim, always a victim? You cannot modify history, so how do you get out of it? It was a long time before she really accepted that no one would ever take me away from her. That sort of imagery stays with you. I was a child who tried to shoulder her mother's catastrophe. I know now what an impossible task I'd set for myself. Yet I would try to do it again, if only I could.

Mutti had a special treat in mind for me. She took me to the movies. I don't remember the film we saw, but I will never forget the newsreel: *The Eyes and Ears of the World*. You would have had to see Mutti's eyes in the flickering light to understand. On the screen were aerial views of Berlin, the still smoking shell of my mother's city. Everything in every direction lay in ruins. I felt Mutti's panic rise in me. On the streets of her neighborhood, a few blocks from the Kurfurstendamm Station, expressionless children, old men, and ragged women stumbled in a daze through the rubble of their homes. On Rosenthalerstrasse in die Mitte, the City Center, the buildings were flattened. There once stood her adorable uncle Heinrich Schlesinger's shirt factory, which made as fine a shirt as could be found in Europe.

Mutti half rose from her seat, gasping, "*Mein Gott, meine Freundinen.* My God, my girlfriends." All at once she realized the danger to old friends she once had in Berlin. "*Nur bloss nicht!* Oh, no, no, the very thought," she cried out. "*Ilonka und Erika.*"

People turned to stare.

"*Mein Gott, mein Gott, Erika und Ilonka. Gott steh dem bei. Erika und Ilonka. Gott steh dem bei.* Oh my God, oh my God, Erica and Ilonka. God stand by them, God stand by them."

A terrible wound in her had reopened. What I saw in her eyes made clear to me the meaning of terror. She stood like a sleepwalker and left the theater, mumbling as a mantra, "Thank God, Ursula is safe in Africa. Thank God, Ursula is safe in Africa, *mit Bruno und Herbert.*"

I followed her out into the sun and took her hand. "Ilonka and Erica. Who are they, Mommy? Who is Ursula? Please tell me. And who are Bruno and Herbert? I want to know."

She nodded as if to acknowledge my right to be told, and she opened her mouth to speak. There, on the crowded street, she held her head in her hands and her lips moved, but no sound issued forth. Mutti, always so proper, tried not at all to conceal this public display of emotion. I knew this was good, for she usually kept her pain inside.

I got her home and sat her down. I was a little girl who well knew how to make a pot of tea, and I poured her a cup. I needed to know. I was insistent to know who those names belonged to. Again and again I asked, to no avail. When night fell, she slipped back into this world again and was calm.

"I sing for you a present," she said apologetically, and she gave me a private little concert of my own, my favorite, "*Der Kleine Sandmann bin Ich.* The Little Sandman Am I."

Abends will ich schlafen geh'n
vierzehn Engel um mich stehn.
When I lay me down to sleep,
fourteen angels watch do keep.

This is the tender lullaby from the opera *Hansel and Gretel* by Engelbert Humperdinck. It had been Mutti's favorite when she was a child. She never forgot the name Humperdinck because her father grieved so terribly for the composer the day he died in 1921.

"I was only six years old, then," she said. "That he felt the loss of Humperdinck so deeply influenced the meaning of music for me ever since. Allow your grandfather's example to so influence you."

She hadn't answered who the names she cried out in the theater belonged to, but she spoke of her father. My grandfather. He taught Mutti as she taught me, to take in music, not with the ears alone but with the heart—an easy lesson because her singing was, for anyone who heard her, a heartfelt joy.

"Thank you for my present. It's the best ever."

"*Nein, nein,*" she said. "Victory in Europe is the best present you will ever get."

I was disappointed. Other children got toys. "The best present I will ever get for the rest of my life?"

"The rest of your life," she said, "is your present."

The meaning was too subtle for the mind of a child, although the words were not too subtle for me to hold in memory more than sixty years later. I could not but measure the relative importance of birthday gifts ever since, against Mutti's astonishing remark. For there are perplexing things in this world that echo inside as special just because they are not understood but felt. Still, I was not too young to understand that the victory in Europe celebrations in the street paled next to her triumph. She had sat by the radio to hear how the Allied armies had prevailed over the liars, the thieves, the murderers. If she was vindicated for the murder of her family and the outrage she had endured, it was a triumph without victory. She had survived, but a lifetime of healing would never make her world whole because of the loss of her loved ones. For all her warmth, for a long time she kept an impenetrable shield around her heart against the dread she learned to expect from the world.

Patriotism and celebration ran high upon the defeat of Germany, and never more so than on that Fourth of July in 1945, though the war in the Pacific did not end until August. The mother next door, Gigi McCoy, would not stand for her new German neighbors spending it alone. She invited us to come to a family barbecue she held in her backyard every year. Mutti spoke only a few words of English. She was reluctant to go, although she knew I would stay close by and interpret as best I could if someone tried to make conversation. She also knew she must reach out, if only for my sake. The aroma of barbecue in the air made an equally convincing argument. We went next door and stepped into a world light years away.

"*Um Gottes willen. Warum stierst du so? Es ist unhöfflich.* Lord's sake, why are you staring? It is impolite," Mutti whispered.

I was gaping at a huge family milling about in their backyard, women busy setting a long table with all the different dishes they had brought, a young man in a sailor suit just home from war, men tending barbecue, brothers and sisters and cousins and kids, one of them named "Corky," playing hide-and-seek and arguing and running everywhere. Cowboys and Indians whooped it up and did their mischief. Loving parents, aunts, and uncles wagged warning fingers, and grandparents reminded them that they, too, once were children.

What is family? The revelation I stared at was family. A big family in the utter pleasure of the company of one another. This is why my first memory of the Fourth stands out. I saw what it meant to have family, to belong, while at the same time the experience threw into sharp contrast that I had missed the great joy of knowing my own. That Fourth of July also stands out because I remember seeing Mutti happy. Swept up in the joy of family gemütlichkeit (coziness), she, for a moment, stepped out of herself. I conjure up her face in the rare light of that day. She didn't know a smile curled her lips and her eyes shone with yearning or that she was gaping, too, at a venerable gray-bearded black great-grandfather as he creaked down on a lawn chair and rested his hands on his cane, adoringly observing the generations of his progeny with pride and satisfaction. How we envied them their family, the old and easy familiarity of shared history.

That Fourth of July, Mutti lived in the fantasy of a ghostly equivalence of a past I knew little of but she knew well, the love that runs wide in a big family circle. For me, such happiness was something new. All the while, our next-door neighbor, Gigi, was radiating love for us. Later, when Mutti was fortunate to find a job, the only one she could, in the home of Otto Preminger as a sleep-in caretaker for his aged mother, Gigi took me in. It was not from Mutti that I learned how to cook. And it was Gigi's son, Corky McCoy, a friend still to this day, who let it be known in the neighborhood that if harm came to a hair on my head, that "fool" would have Corky to contend with. No small matter.

All of this set our loss fresh in front of us. The war had torpedoed Mutti's ship of life and sent it to the bottom, and with it her history. She had not even a photograph of her parents to cherish. Peace left us marooned, without linkage to a past. We were physically safe now in America, but what of the psyche? What safe haven exists to balance the mind? My mother was a gentle woman for whom the very idea of hatred and violence was bewildering. She saw it, knew it, felt it, but never quite grasped how such a phenomenon could be. How to undo the psychic poison of years of persecution and the unrelenting daily dread of wondering about her brother, Mops, and the family she'd left at home in Germany? As for her father and mother, she knew all along what had happened to them. Going through Mutti's papers after she died, I came across a German Red Cross letter from my Uncle Mops, dated September 13, 1942, which allowed the sending of no more than twenty-five abbreviated words:

"This morning, on my [twenty-second] birthday, [our] parents 'have traveled,' destination unknown. No change [for the] better. Friends and little girlfriend help touchingly. [Just the same] I hold [my] head [up] high. Write to me. Your Ernst."

Mutti never told me of this letter. There were two more letters from Mops before they stopped coming. Who would want to tell their child such a thing? And no wonder. I never have been able to push away morbid thoughts of what happened to my grandparents on that morning. The professor, the favorite of his students, among whom were more than a few Nazis, proud soldier in the army of the Kaiser, hears a pounding on his door by his fellow citizens garbed in the same uniform he once wore and with his wife, Paula, is thrown helpless to the street and forced to march in front of their neighbors

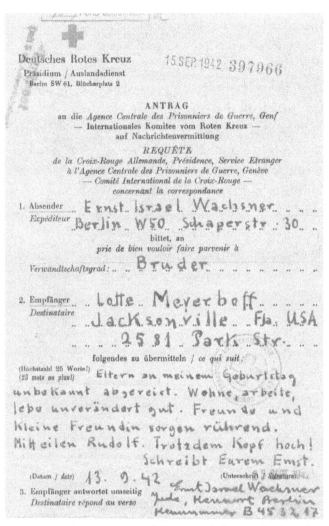

The Red Cross letter from my uncle Mops in which my mother learned her parents' fates. She never told me of the letter.

in a tragic parade through Berlin to the Anhalter train station to be "sent east" in boxcars as cattle to a sadistic slaughter.

How far down can one fall into hell when shocked out of the ideals of a lifetime, which are shown to be an illusion, when the safety net of a caring world is unmasked as a sham, as only a veneer the human race uses to delude itself into believing it isn't savage? How to imagine being caught in a trap with no rights, living among once fellow citizens who are encouraged to hate and revile you and don't want you to stay but won't let you go. How to climb back up to God and find faith again in the society of humans?

Later, I remembered the Germans who went against the socially encouraged hatred of the Jews and put themselves in harm's way. I wonder what kind of immunity they had to protect themselves from the propaganda, what kind of mettle it took for them to expose themselves in a public way to the possibility of dire punishment, when so very many others did not. The mental scars Mutti carried with her were not so tidily erased by physical safety. Nor, I have come to understand, were mine. My identity went to the bottom with hers. All she had left of Germany were the ghosts of her family. She believed her German roots were dead and gone from this world forever.

CHAPTER 2

The Past Disinterred

LIFE HELD NOTHING MORE THAN the sadness I shared in Lotte's eyes. Then came a life-affirming event that had an overwhelming counterbalancing effect on both of us. We were about to discover that during the tragic interlude, Lotte's German roots had not been eradicated but had grown deeper.

One day a huge carton arrived at our door. Something tangible had come from that ever-mysterious homeland of Mutti's called Germany in that far-off continent called Europe. But if the carton was real, the world it came from existed in memory alone. The delivery man struggled to get it into the garage, it was so big. Tattered and frayed, it had clearly been long in transit and had come from far away. It crashed through Lotte's veil of silence. It overwhelmed us. You might say it came from the past, which she could no longer push away, for now the past was sitting before us in a huge carton with her name on it, Charlotte Wachsner Meyerhoff. In my mind's eye, I see it still, sitting in the middle of the cement floor like an oversized piece of furniture. I had to stand on my tiptoes to see over the top of it. Lotte took tentative steps and stood beside me, reading the label with the strange and beautiful handwriting.

"*Ilonka! Du lieber Gott,* dear God," she cried out and backed away from the mysterious package. There it was again, a name I had heard her cry out in the theater.

"Who is Ilonka, Mommy? Tell me."

Mutti seemed not to hear.

"I want to know." I kept it up until this time she answered me.

"Thank God, she is alive. Ilonka was a dear friend of mine in Berlin."

"What has she sent you?"

The question shocked her, as if she herself had not yet thought to wonder and raise to consciousness an answer both dreadful and marvelous. Hours passed. The next day passed. My eyes hardly left the mythic carton as it grew larger and larger, while Lotte pretended it wasn't there at all, as if that would make it grow smaller and disappear.

Then came a crack in the wall she had built around herself. Something fundamental in her shifted, and she could pretend no longer. She found the resolution to deal with it and throw open the window to everything she had tried with all her might to shut away. The arrival of the carton opened the way for her to begin to heal a little. Now she had to come to terms with a past that, despite her best efforts to bury it, had disinterred itself before her. She ventured to the package and began, knot by knot, to untie the strong twine. As in a ritual, she rolled up the twine and set it aside like a holy relic. She began to remove the heavy wrapping paper, taking care not to tear it any more than it had become ragged through weeks of transit. She came to a cardboard box, and I held my breath as she opened the lid. Inside were beautifully pleated layers of tissue tied lovingly with ribbons.

"In Berlin before the war, Ilonka's birthday gifts to me were wrapped this way. Christmas, too." She cried as she untied the ribbons and pulled back the tissue. On top was an envelope. Mutti picked it up with both hands as if it were a priceless artifact newly uncovered at an archaeological dig. Inside was a letter and a little snapshot of a woman dressed in a long white dress with sleeves of lace, holding in her arms a baby also swaddled in long white lace. I thought how beautiful the lady in the picture was. I still have that photograph.

The photo of Ursula with baby Jochen that came in the carton from my mother's friends Ilonka and Erica.

Mutti read the letter again and again. "Ilonka and Erica and Ursula have sent this to me. I cannot imagine."

Those were three of the names she had cried out in the theater. An interminable time passed as she read and reread the letter before turning her attention to the photograph. Such was the fascination it held for her that her eyes froze on it, too. And I remember how it seemed a triumph of will when, at last, she tore them away and stared far off into empty space. She had a way, sometimes, of doing that, as if her eyes still fastened on long-gone images.

"*Nur erst gestern,*" she murmured. "Only yesterday." I badgered Mutti to tell me about the beautiful lady in the picture and the baby in her arms.

"Ma-ri-an-na," she relented at last, "she is Ursula, my friend. We were schoolgirls together in Berlin. *Nur erst gestern.* Only yesterday."

"Tell me about the baby."

21

"*Ja*, the letter says his name is Joachim and he was born in 1939. *Ach, mein Gott*, Ursula's child. Is he not a lovely baby? The picture was taken in Tanganyika when he was born. But, Ma-ri-an-na, he is no longer an infant. He is now six years old. Two years older than you."

We were to learn that Ursula and Bruno had other children. There was Eva, the oldest. Then came Joachim, known affectionately as Jochen, after which the twins, Gisele and Christel, were born, followed by two more sons yet to be conceived. But baby Jochen lived in my mind. I had seen his picture.

"Where is Tanganyika, Mutti?"

"It is in Africa, Ma-ri-an-na. Far, far from Deutschland, as far away as we are in America. *Nur erst gestern*," her lips moved.

She reached inside the carton, took out an object, and began to remove the tissue but stopped, for suddenly her fingers informed her of what was beneath the wrapping that she held in her hands.

"*Unmöglich!*" she cried. "Impossible!" She held it out to me. Her hand was shaking. "You remove, Ma-ri-an-na."

I took it from her and unwrapped it.

"It's beautiful, Mommy," I said of the gleaming treasure I held in my hands. "Who sent us this?"

It was a beautifully wrought old silver box. I could not tear my eyes away from its powerful attraction, as if staring at it long enough would reveal its secret to me. More than sixty years have passed and still I stare in awe at it.

"It is an *etrog* box," she whispered, "used in the Jewish harvest festival of Succot, the Feast of Tabernacles. I thought I would surely not see it again. It is hundreds of years old, my father's most precious possession. My grandfather Siegfried bequeathed it to him, as had his father, Isaac, before him."

This rare artifact of Judaica had been handed down in my family from father to son for nearly two centuries, as far back as could be traced. Why do I remember that the moment I touched it, the *etrog* box felt warm to me, as if hands that long held it had just let go? I held it up to her to give it back. Instead, Mutti took my hands, still holding the box, in hers.

The beautiful, and very old, silver etrog box we found in the carton from Germany.

"My father," she said proudly, oblivious of her tears. "Doktor Fritz Wachsner, professor of chemistry and biology. A German man. A Jewish man. A most wonderful father and soldier for Deutschland. At home, my brother and I called him 'Der Alte Fritz,' 'Old Man Fritz,' but you had better watch out. If he heard us call him that, he would chase us around the house until he caught us."

Her description of him frightened me.

"Mommy, what did he do when he caught you?"

"He tickled us because, although he was a stern disciplinarian, his science insisted the equation didn't work unless he was equally a mischievous disciplinarian. He was so alive, Ma-ri-an-na. You have so much to be proud of." Then she let go of my hands while I still held the *etrog* box.

Next, Mutti took out a cloth bag that held exquisitely carved antique Christmas tree ornaments and clips for fastening live candles to the tree.

"Klarchen," she whispered, shaking her head.

She looked long and hard at each of them, revisiting memories she was not ready to share. Then she took out a pair of silver Regency candlesticks that held the tapers Jewish women light every Friday night to welcome the Sabbath into their homes. They had graced the Wachsner dining room table in Berlin for as long as Mutti could remember.

The silver candlesticks that had graced the Wachsner dining table in Berlin and now are on my table in California.

Now they are on my table in California. I am staring at them as I write. Each time my eyes fall upon them, my mind flashes back to the daunting moment when Mutti took them out of the carton, for again she withdrew from the solemn reality of it all and fell mute. It seemed hours that she sat staring into space. I like to think that the vision before her eyes was of her family who, scant years earlier, had sat with her around a Sabbath table illuminated by these very same candlesticks, her stepmother Paula's hands hovering in benediction above the flames.

In the carton were also a few old pieces of family jewelry whose greatest value lies in my having learned the names of my grandmothers who once wore them. These were objects of earthly beauty, but the carton contained a much greater treasure. There were more than a thousand old documents, family letters, wedding announcements, my grandfather's first report cards and graduation certificates, university records, diplomas, postcards, and diaries. There were photograph albums, some with pictures of my family dating back to the nineteenth century when cameras were new. Mutti took pleasure in showing me the pictures and telling me the names of the faces she recognized until I came to know them as real people. In this way she continued to open herself and me to the past, and so to a future.

There was also a manuscript dated 1935, written by my grand-father, with the title *Gotteskampf!* (God's Struggle), unpublished, of course, in which he pleads the rights of Germans who happened to be Jews, while admonishing them never to forget their born duty to the ideals of "*Judentum und Deutschtum*," Judaism and Germanness. How could he have displayed the courage, in days such as those, to use that title? It was clearly a play on *Mein Kampf*, trumping Hitler's struggle with God's.

Resolutely, Mutti packed up all the letters and the documents and put them away on the top shelf of her wardrobe. For her to know where they were and that they were safe in her possession was enough. She never looked at them again. It was just too much. But for me, the carton held far more than the sum of its contents. The pictures of my family, my people who had touched these things, were like the con-tents of a time capsule. A window to the past had opened through which I could look back directly upon the broken life our family had lived and the friends who once populated my mother's world. These were the people she belonged to and about whom until then she had told me so little. The arrival of the carton was a rite of passage. My total lack of identity, of belonging and roots, had been abruptly jux-taposed by a centuries-old archive of my family in Germany, dropped into our laps from out of the past. But dropped by whom?

"My girlfriends, my dearest girlfriends, Ilonka and Erica and Ursula," she said. Her eyes revealed the proper place in her heart she now restored them to, a place where they had been all along.

I wanted to know everything about them so they could occupy the same place in mine. Now Mutti began to release a little about the years before I was born and how she came to befriend the three girls in Berlin who were more her sisters than her friends. But there were other names she had cried out in the theater. Men's names, Bruno and Herbert. Who were they?

Lotte answered with a love story.

Ursula was the first of the four girls to fall in love, and Bruno Namgalies became her betrothed. He was studying to be a clergyman when they met, and he was ordained into the Lutheran ministry not long after Hitler came to power. In 1935, the church offered him and his best friend and fellow seminarian Herbert Bahr missionary posts in Africa. The men did not have to think twice. Bruno and Ursula went off together to be wed in Tanganyika, where they took up their missionary duties. As for Herbert Bahr, he went, too, but with a heavy heart. The woman he loved, whom he hoped would share his life, remained behind in Berlin.

"Bruno and Herbert knew what others should have but did not."

I was in my teens when this comment fell from Mutti's lips out of nowhere. By "others," perhaps she meant my grandfather, Der Alte Fritz, who could have left before it was too late, but he was the head of an extended family that he could neither arrange to take with him nor bear to leave behind. Perhaps she meant that all the Jews of Germany should have taken Hitler at his word. Her comment would have applied just as well if she had meant the whole of the German people. So many of them, if never a majority, had gone over to Hitler, some among Mutti's own friends who thought his racial theories absurd and Nazism just a short, necessary deal with the devil, a political phase to pull the country together, a transition that in time would fall away of itself. Support for Nazism was much wider than it was deep, but the day was fast approaching when Germans of every stripe would come to know what "Bruno and Herbert knew," that once Hitler was given power, it was already too late. He swiftly seized control over every single part of life in Germany, even twisting religion to his will.

"Those who disagreed found it wiser to keep their mouths shut," Mutti said, "leaving the Neanderthals to do all the barking. Without freedom of conscience in Germany, they could not have preached in good faith. Bruno and Ursula and Herbert would have none of this nonsense. Nineteen thirty-five was a good time to get out of Germany. It was a sad farewell.

"So, now the war is over and Ursula and Bruno have returned from Africa. They have brought their young family home to Deutschland."

Lotte didn't know there was aching in the way the words *family*, *home*, and *Deutschland* came out of her mouth or that she shuddered each time she murmured, "*Nur erst gestern*. Only yesterday." The child that I was understood the *Klangfarb*, the nuance in her voice. It came with mother's milk. "Only yesterday" meant a lifetime ago.

In the midst of these ruminations, Lotte was suddenly exhausted. Later that night, when she thought I was asleep, she read Ilonka's letter again and again while she sobbed into her pillow until, in the wee hours of the morning, she fell asleep.

Lotte saved the empty carton and the twine. The next day we took her shopping cart and went to every grocery store within walking distance, looking for food of the sort she rarely bought for us, much of which was still hard to find on American shelves in the immediate postwar period.

"This we send to Deutschland, for they have no food, and Ursula alone has many mouths to feed."

"Ursula with the blue eyes and golden braids?"

"She is prettier than her picture," Lotte said. "Hair like flax. Skin like milk, and the tiniest of waists."

Years later, when I was older, she happened to share a memory of Ursula that brought a spontaneous smile to her face. "We were shopping at Ka De We, the most wonderful department store in all Berlin, when we heard a military band coming down Kurfurstendamm. The doors to the store swung wildly, and suddenly the store began flooding with pedestrians from the street. The Gestapo soon followed the people in and they indiscriminately herded everybody, customers and clerks alike, back out onto the sidewalk, emptying the first floor of the store. We found ourselves pushed to the curb as a long troop of Hitler Jugend came parading by. A standardbearer stepped smartly by us. All raised our arms in the Nazi salute. Just then, the standardbearer caught sight of Ursula from the corner of his eye and tripped on the heels of the boy marching in front of him. It was a very clumsy stumble," she said. "It was very funny. No one laughed. He must have earned a harsh reprimand."

Lotte (left), with Erica (center) and Ursula (right).

Ursula Bauze in the 1930s.

28

Lotte (seated, right), age fifteen, with her lute at the Elisabeth Christinen Lyceum School in Berlin, 1930. Erica is seated next to her.

Ilonka, 1938.

We came home exhausted, with the grocery cart filled to the brim and our arms laden with more. There were cans of fruits, vegetables, ham, chicken, and tuna; packages of Jell-O and puddings; dry milk, pounds of sugar, rice, and flour; olive oil; chocolate bars; and other wonders. Mutti packed it all up in the same empty carton we had just gotten from Berlin and put my picture on top, and tied it with the original twine. Mr. Rodia came with his old, battered truck to pick us up and take us downtown to the Red Cross office to ship the carton to Germany.

So it was that our care package, the first of many, went from Lotte's heart to her Christian friends in the same spirit of the incomparable treasure they had kept and preserved for her, the gift of memory and connection. I asked her how her friends came to possess all the things they sent. She was pensive, gloomy, then shook her head as if to shake away the grim thought.

"I dare not think," she said. "It could only be that my parents gave them these things. *Meine lieben Freundinen.* My dear girlfriends kept them for me. It is *unglaublich,* unbelievable."

The power of the carton was not in its contents alone but in the timing of its arrival. Lotte thought her roots in Germany had been severed. When the carton came unexpectedly into our lives, she discovered that the stem had been cut, but the roots had only grown deeper to flower again. A missing piece of her identity had been restored. Her girlfriends hadn't forgotten her. In that miraculous moment and by that slender thread, she was reunited with a lost part of her heart.

The war was over and mail had just started to be delivered between Europe and America, so Mutti wrote to her girlfriends and resumed her friendship, interrupted, not ended, by the war. These women grew to be legends to me. Their correspondence lasted throughout their lifetimes.

The child I was thought that if only I had friends like Lotte's, if only I, too, belonged, how happy I would be, so I made her heart connections my legends. If their arms could open that wide for Lotte, surely there was room in their embrace for me, just because I was her daughter.

The photo of me that Mutti put in the first care package we sent to Germany.

There was more to the story of the romance of Ursula and Bruno, for conjoined to their love was a love of Mutti's own, none other than Bruno's fellow seminarian Herbert Bahr. Lotte and Herbert and Ursula and Bruno. The four were inseparable. Years were to pass before I learned how Mutti's and Herbert's broken hearts played out against Ursula and Bruno's happy betrothal in those early years following Hitler's appointment as chancellor. It was not Mutti who told me this part of the story. It came from Ursula herself when I met her, years later.

As I grew up, I came to learn from Mutti how the four girls first met. On my mother's sixth birthday my grandfather announced to the family that she was to have a career in music, and she began to study voice and piano. Paula, her stepmother, was a fabulous cook, but Mutti's father would not let Paula teach her.

"A person can sing but she must also eat," Paula said extra loudly so Der Alte Fritz was sure to hear. "If she expects to eat and feed her family, a woman must first learn how to cook. And if she would cook, she must learn how to boil water."

Der Alte Fritz's answer never wavered. "Do not let Lotte near the kitchen. She has a remarkable instrument that must be developed. She is meant to be a great artist."

"Papa had spoken," Mutti said. "He found my first teacher."

When Mutti turned fifteen in 1930, her father deemed her ready to be groomed by a major teacher who would take her on for professional training. He heard of an up-and-coming young teacher in Berlin, none other than Ilonka Von Patti. She was only in her thirties but enjoyed a burgeoning reputation as a distinguished teacher of voice. She had been a wunderkind and looked not all that much older than Mutti. Student hopefuls came from all over to seek her advice. She took only the most promising. It was hard to get an appointment, but she, in turn, had heard of Doktor Wachsner, whose name was almost as familiar in music circles as in academia.

"I was shaking with embarrassment when your grandfather took me to meet her because I knew it was his reputation alone that got me through the door. I felt unworthy."

Mutti was struck with the instant authority Ilonka projected, and Ilonka had little patience.

"Well, then, what will you sing for me today, Fräulein Wachsner?"

" 'Ye Who Know Sorrow,' " Mutti replied.

This astonished Ilonka. "From Johannes Brahms's *Ein Deutsches Requiem*, you mean to say? Don't you think that a bit ambitious, Herr Doktor?"

"Papa just smiled. His confidence was greater than mine."

"*Na ja*, well, yes," he answered, "but is it not ambition that brings us here today, Fräulein Von Patti?" Charmer that he was, his grin suggested he knew something that she did not.

"Perhaps she can show me the voice. We shall see. But what can a child know of the sorrow? All right then, sing," demanded Ilonka.

Hardly had Mutti opened her mouth when Ilonka stopped her.

"You screech like an alley cat. Not from the throat. Have you not learned to sing from the diaphragm?"

Mutti was mortified with embarrassment and thought that Ilonka would show them out. "I looked to my father for help, but he only winked at me with his subtle Wachsner smile."

"Now, then," Ilonka said, "once again, if you will."

"And suddenly it came to me," Mutti said, "that my first lesson with Ilonka Von Patti had already begun."

Something transcendental happened between Ilonka and Mutti that magical day. Teacher and student bonded completely. A few years later, when Mutti's career began to blossom, Ilonka confessed to my grandfather that she had heard from the very first note the dormant beauty of Mutti's voice, that a student hopeful with her potential, needing only to be released by the training that Ilonka was eager to provide, was what she herself had always searched for. Ilonka became more than a teacher; she was a mentor and a friend. Soon they were going to recitals, concerts, and even jazz clubs and cabarets to listen to chanteuses. They attended a performance of Ernst Toch's Piano Concerto at the Berlin Philharmonic.

"Hear the dissonance not with your ears alone, but visualize it as blades of grass moving in a random breeze. Allow the contemporary sound to build a path in you in heart and mind, the better to listen and to widen how you take in the classical and romantic composers you already adore, Bach and Haydn and Beethoven and Brahms, Mendelssohn, Schubert, Schumann, Liszt and Wagner and Strauss and Bruckner and Mahler."

They regularly attended the Berlin State Opera, where Ilonka explained the meaning and the nuances of the hand signals and arm movements with which the conductor, Otto Klemperer, directed the orchestra.

Lotte knew that one's parents tend to overestimate the talent of their children, but Ilonka's belief in her confirmed that she might become a good singer. Ilonka gave her the confidence to try seriously for a career.

On the day of Mutti's audition, Erica, who was also a pupil of Ilonka's, was waiting in the anteroom for her lesson to begin. She was a supremely gifted alto with equal talent as a pianist.

"Erica. Dear, dear Erica Poch," Mutti said. "I met her in Ilonka's studio. I was on my way out with my father when I saw her for the first time. We often ran into each other at Ilonka's. It wasn't long before we discovered that we attended the same Gymnasium, Elisabeth Christinen Lyceum. Erica was so mischievous. She loved having a good time, and believe me, Berlin was the town, in those days, for having a good time. You must understand that Erica had a mind of her own, forthright, headstrong, outspoken. But then, she was a Berlinerin, *Liebchen*. And Berlin was a different world than anyplace else in Deutschland."

It was there at school that Erica introduced Mutti to her friend, their fellow student Ursula Bautze, beautiful Ursula with the blue eyes, long golden braids, and tiny waist, who aspired to be a great painter.

"We were happy to find that, coincidentally, our parents all knew each other, which tied us together in an unexpected way. We enjoyed very much that they were friends, too. In time, we came to believe that like sisters, we were preordained to meet. We could be quite the cutups.

"But then the Nazis took over and we began to feel *Gleichschaltung* in our bones. Ilonka readily found approval from high-ranking, newly enriched Nazi Party members who could now afford to impose the best training for their children on her. As for Ursula, she found approval as the spitting image of Hitler's idea of a *Völkisch Mädchen* (a racially pure Aryan girl). But Erica walked a fine line when the Nazis came to power. Her personality traits were not the ones the Party found attractive in a German girl. And certainly mine weren't, either."

Lotte had trouble translating *Gleichschaltung* for me and grappled with it a while. Then, as always, she consulted her German-English dictionary and explained that it meant Nazification, pronouncing the word as best she could. "The forced and mindless joining in lockstep with the crowd," she called it.

"If there was anything Erica was not, it was a conformist. I begged her to be careful, to keep silent, but she was not afraid. Ilonka and Ursula, too. They were not afraid. I was afraid enough for the four of us. I didn't want to get them in trouble."

"Afraid of what?" I asked.

"*Du muss ein bisschen alter seine,*" she said. "When you are a little older."

In those years before 1933 and afterward, the four women created a loyalty that was never broken by subsequent events.

"*Wir waren 'die Vier Freundinen aus Berlin,'*" Lotte said. "We called ourselves '*die VFB.*'"

My eighteenth birthday was special. Lotte wished she could throw me the kind of birthday party Paula had for her when she came of age, but that was impossible since nobody cooked or baked more dazzlingly delicious dinners than Paula did, most certainly not Mutti.

"It is a pity. I miss German cooking. I wish I knew her recipes."

So Mutti took me out for my birthday to Van de Kamp's restaurant on the Miracle Mile for a fish-and-chips dinner. She poked at her salad, but nourishment for her meant the usual cup of coffee, piece of pie, and cigarettes. I watched her puff away on her umpteenth cigarette.

"*Die Vier Berlinerinen,*" Lotte said. "I talk about any one of us and soon I am talking of all four. *Ja, wir waren die Vier liebe Freundinen.* We four were the dearest of girlfriends." She put it differently sometimes: "*Wir waren die Vier Berlinerinen.* We were the Four Girls from Berlin."

I heard no distinction in either case and took her to mean the girls were all for one and one for all. Yet the second way was a code that held a subtle but vastly different shade of meaning. I didn't understand this until she let me know on my birthday at Van de Kamp's. I don't know why she chose this birthday to tell me—maybe because I was now the same age that she had been at the time. Or perhaps she had traveled enough emotional distance from those wonderful, terrible days to loosen the reins she held on her silence. It may have been a futile attempt once again to make sense of it all, having long ago come to understand that no amount of insight could shed ultimate light on the Holocaust. Yet tell it she must, especially when there were good and noble things to remember, as well as the bad.

"All the boys were signing up for the Hitler Youth. Girls were joining the girls' parallel, *die Bund Deutsches Mädchens, die BDM,* the League of German Girls. They made you out to be unpatriotic if you did not."

Erica couldn't decide whether to spit in their faces or cut her own throat if forced to join an organization that trumpeted such stupidity. It wasn't long before she had her chance.

"Erica and Ursula and I were coming down the street one day, and a group of BDM girls came over and asked us where our badges were. Why hadn't we joined? I was frightened to death. Was I supposed to tell them I hadn't joined *die BDM* because I was a Jew? Erica stepped in and saved us from a scene, and she did not have to spit in their faces or cut her throat to do it.

"'We don't need to join up,' she told the girls, talking down to them. 'Didn't you know?' she asked, her voice turning confidential. 'We already belong to *die DDB*.' Not chancing to look stupid and inquire further, the girls walked on. So it was for us to ask Erica just what in heaven's name *die DDB* stood for.

"'It means, the three of us. I told them we belong to 'the three of us.' *Die Drei Berlinerinen, die DDB*. The Three Girls from Berlin. Our own secret little bund.' We had a very unhappy laugh, while they each took my arm and told me how ashamed they were and hurt for me, that the disgrace belonged to the Nazis for their insults, not to me, and that they were devoted and respected me and loved me, and surely our Fatherland would soon come to its senses and throw the crazies out of office."

Ursula told Mutti that she and Erica would never have grown to be such close friends if it weren't for Mutti.

"Since you have come into the picture, you are the one around whom all of us flutter."

Lotte denied it, but Erica agreed. If anything, Hitler had brought them closer to rally around her.

"It wasn't long before the inevitable happened. Someone overheard us blaspheme Nazism. Spies were everywhere, especially among our fellow students, who reported anything you said to the Gestapo and the SS. We were lucky this time. It was Ilonka who heard, and she was angry with us. For a moment I thought the impossible, that she was one of them. She put a finger to her lips and told us we had to be much more careful about what came out of our mouths.

"'How do you know? Suppose I was a party member? You would be far over your heads in trouble.' But many of Ilonka's friends in the world of music were Jews. Her own mentor was Jewish. She had her own ax to grind.'"

"Who is in charge of the Membership Committee of your secret little bund?" Ilonka asked. And thus was born *die Vier Berlinerinen*, the Four Girls from Berlin.

Lotte was "discovered" at Ilonka's studio. The renowned Richard Tauber heard her sing the Beethoven lied "Adelaide" and was stunned. Lotte would learn stagecraft from the great German tenor while helping him to prepare for concerts and personal appearances. She would sing with him in practice sessions, in duets, and at rehearsals. Others now would hear her. It was a coveted opportunity among young hopefuls of Berlin, where music, still to this day, is as basic as bread. In time, she appeared on stage with him and was on her way to a promising career as a mezzo-soprano, but it wasn't long before the Nazis put an end to it. Who could have predicted that her budding career would not be permitted to flower, and that the magnificent voice of Richard Tauber as well would soon be silenced in Germany?

One Sunday I heard my mother sing before an audience for the first time, at a party at Lotte Lehman's School of Music in Santa Barbara. I was five or six years old. Among the guests were many native German speakers, expatriates who were doing their level best to speak only English, especially to one another.

Mutti was oblivious of the fact that her demeanor had changed the moment we came through the door, as if her autonomic nervous system had overcome a long hypnotic spell and brought her back to the erased milieu of her former life. As she moved among the guests, I glimpsed something I had not seen in her before, the unassuming social ease and self-confidence she must have exuded in her natural habitat as a poised young woman of Berlin. She began to sing. It took but a moment for a hush to fall over the room. Her voice was astonishing, commanding your attention. It was not simply a matter of producing beautiful tones. Her voice seemed to waft like a breeze, as if disconnected from its source, and hang suspended in midair. An effortless voice, a pure voice with unadorned phrasing, trained to hold its power in never-called-upon reserve.

I talk in vain. Words cannot represent what only the ears are meant to discern. Sometimes a certain magic, a symbiosis, is created between an artist and an audience of many, a much different experience from when Mutti sang to me alone. I saw her now through new eyes, and always since, as Mutti, a commanding presence, an artist of stature, torn from her moorings and dispossessed but ever the lady of grandeur. Our hostess, Lotte Lehman, sat down beside me. Mutti knew her as a friend of my grandparents in Berlin.

"Ma-ri-an-na," she said, "you must be a very proud little girl."

"This is how proud," I replied. "When I hear music I think of my Mutti, and when I think of my Mutti, I hear music."

I know she told my mother, for anytime we had a "misunderstanding," Mutti reminded me of what I had said to Lotte Lehman that day.

Afterward, we walked around beautiful Santa Barbara until it was time to board the Los Angeles bus. Mutti took me to an ice cream store and told me I could have anything I wanted. We both had sugar cones with two scoops. The day had released an old side of Lotte, a mood of lightness and spontaneity that I adored. We were giddy and laughing on the bus and when we got home. Exhaustion and escaping to sleep was how Mutti ended a day that had immersed her in the past. She had expunged much.

What I said to Lotte Lehman is still true. Mutti's voice was the best part of my childhood. I wish I could hear her sing again now. Whoever heard her sing felt that way. But her father was no longer there to guide her, and her health was too poor to sustain an operatic career. She was in America ten years before she became a nurse.

CHAPTER 3

Benny and Daddy

COUNTLESS THOUSANDS OF THE HOMELESS, still unaccounted for, were roaming Europe or living in displaced persons camps. Thus it was a miracle when a very special letter from England tracked us down through the International Red Cross. I remember the odd way Lotte held the envelope away from herself as if to hand the matter over to the Invisible One Who had the power to bless and make good the news it contained. She tore it open. Inside she found another envelope, and on it was the handwriting of the sublime personage of none other than Rabbi Benno Gottschalk. She gasped as she opened the second envelope carefully so as not to harm something precious his hands had last touched. The rabbi was writing to let her know he had gotten out of Germany and survived the war in England.

He had been warned by a "friend" in the Gestapo that he had just one day to get out of Germany or suffer dire consequences. This was at the very moment his wife had been hospitalized and could not be moved. He had no choice but to leave her behind, along with every-thing he owned. In England, with no assets, he did all in his power to bring her there, but by the time she could travel, the door had slammed shut.

Rabbi Benno Gottschalk, 1938.

The rabbi was German to the core, but his Germany, his Berlin, his congregation and temple and way of life were no more. Lotte wrote to him, imploring him to come to California. If there was any-place on earth he belonged, it was in America with us.

Mutti could hand sew beautifully, and she made me an outfit with a little hat to match, to wear on the day of the rabbi's arrival. I still feel her clutching my hand high above my head as the train chugged into Union Station. It began to disgorge its passengers. She scruti-nized the faces and scanned the platform, but where was the dashing Rabbi Gottschalk? An old man whose eyes came to rest on Mutti stood at the door of a carriage. His gaze shifted to me and frightened me. It was hard for him to step onto the platform. He shuffled halt-ingly toward us. It was only then that Mutti turned and saw the frail and bent *alter* approaching. She was shocked. In the seven years since she had seen him last, he had aged beyond his years and was now but an apparition of his old self. She gathered him into her arms, fight-ing back an irrepressible need to weep.

"You don't recognize me anymore, but I knew you right away, dear Lotte. And this is little Ma-ri-an-na."

Mutti pulled me in with them. No arm's length here. He asked about my grandfather and Paula. She told him only that the last let-

Rabbi Gottschalk (standing, second from left) with members of his Reform congregation in Berlin, 1935.

ter she had sent them was returned, stamped "Addressee unknown," and she knew nothing about the fate of Mops. As for the rest of the family, she didn't think anyone had survived. What the rabbi said to me then I'll never forget.

"Your grandfather wrote to me to tell me you were born. He was never so happy. Listen well, little girl, and remember. In you has your whole family been redeemed."

He bent down and opened his arms to me. I hid behind Mutti. I still wonder why. Perhaps I resented even then the immense weight of being called upon to fulfill the promise of all those lives cut short.

We walked home from the bus, and Mutti and he took turns carrying his suitcase. When we turned onto our street and came up the path to the garage, it was the rabbi's turn to be shocked. The last time he had seen my mother was at the Berlin home of her parents in 1938 when he officiated at her wedding. Mutti followed his gaze to the garage. Her eyes opened wide, as if her veil of guilt for still being alive lifted for a moment and she could glimpse for the first time the indigence of the home she had made.

In time, the rabbi would get his *Wiedergutmachen* from the government of Germany and would find a better place for us to live. The literal translation of the word is "to make good again." The mind of a child could not quite get hold of the sense of it. How in the world could what happened be "made good again"? I asked Lotte what the word was in English. She looked up the translation in her German-English dictionary.

"To make restitution," she said, means "to right a wrong."

I'm still struck by the relative etymology of the two words. How the same thought comes down in modern languages tells you something about the psychic disposition of different peoples. The English phrase "to right a wrong" means to make whole again, not "to make good again," as in the German. Neither are possible since that which is unrecoverable can't be restored. But *restitution* implies an attempt in earnest to dole out justice to the victims and right a wrong. *Wiedergutmachen* has the smack of doling out recompense in order that the wrongdoer is made to feel "good again." Dragging of heels and making the injured jump through hoops for years, waiting for their *Wiedergutmachen*, and if they lived that long, to get back a small portion of what had been stolen, may be another symptom of this mindset. In the case of Rabbi Gottschalk, when he did receive his *Wiedergutmachen*, it was a great deal of money, though a fraction of the value of his confiscated estate.

Before he got his *Wiedergutmachen*, he needed a job, anything to create income. Indomitable Benny, hobbled though he was, went downtown and found work delivering telegrams for Western Union. We pooled our meager assets and rented a modest, though proper, apartment. He went with us on Sundays to the Unitarian church, until members of the German colony in Los Angeles discovered he was there and formed a congregation around him. Reverend Fritchman was charmed by him and felt honored that Rabbi Gottschalk of Berlin came to his services. They took pleasure in each other's company and began a friendship in which the spiritual and the metaphysical implications of how mankind comports itself in the world was a constant topic of discussion. Benny's wisdom had a powerful formative influence upon me as I grew up. Now I, too, had a grandfather.

But where was my father? That far-off, make-believe world Mutti called *die Zukunft*, "the future," when the war would end, had passed, but my father did not come home. Day after day we waited for word and heard nothing. Then at last a letter came. Mutti's hands shook when she saw the handwriting on the envelope.

"It is from Germany, from your father," she said. "Look, he has written your name, too. It is addressed to Mrs. Charlotte Meyerhoff and Ma-ri-an-na Meyerhoff."

An unfamiliar sense of pride and status rose up in me as my mother tore open the envelope. I watched her as she read the letter, and I could read its contents in the disappointment in her eyes. She pinched them closed to compose herself, then opened them and smiled brightly at me. Benny and I could always tell that something was wrong when she put on her best face for us, underneath which I felt her helplessness every time. I smiled back to sustain the charade and thought, Mommy, I know you are frightened and for that you are all the braver and dearer to me.

"Your father must remain in Germany in the Army of Occupation." She looked embarrassed, as if she were somehow to blame.

"*Warum, Mutti*, but why?" I pleaded.

She shrugged and sighed and cupped my chin in her hand. "Perhaps so that in time, Deutschland can be made to heal."

She turned back to the letter. In Berlin, Daddy had discovered that on September 13, 1942, Fritz and Paula Wachsner had been deported to Riga and put to death upon arrival. She had surmised the worst when Mops, on his twenty-second birthday, wrote to her that they had been taken away. She kept it bottled up then, but now it was public property and Mutti's strength drained out of her. The letter fell from her hands and she erupted in an unconsolable burst of tears. Just to hear her weep had me crying, too. This startled her. I have always wondered why. Could she not have known this was my tragedy, too?

"What they have done, it can never be healed," Mutti said when she had no more tears to shed.

"But not all of them, Mutti. There are those who are good. You said so yourself."

Lotte smiled the smile of the forlorn. What else to do with love and grief smothered by outrage but to release it with a smile when there can be no "making good" again?

"*Danke, mein liebes Kind. Nein, nein.* Thank you, my dear child. Most certainly not all of them."

Benny struggled to force down his own tears. He picked up the letter and put it back in her hand. It said that Mops had been hiding underground in Berlin throughout the war and was last seen when the city fell, present whereabouts unknown. Mops was in that religious stage of adolescence and thinking of becoming a rabbi just as Hitler became chancellor. Perhaps he would have, perhaps not. One thing was certain: his timing was poor.

Mutti's grief was buffered by the possibility of being reunited with Mops. For a moment, her hopes soared. But where was he? A conflicting report sent our spirits crashing. Mops, it said, had been captured in Berlin by the Gestapo and sent to Auschwitz. A third report said "Fate unknown." The trail so far led to a dead end. All the same, there was an outside chance that he was alive somewhere. The odds were not good, but it was all we had to pin our hopes on. Daddy would continue to try. I never told Mutti what I learned about Onkel Mops's fate from an eyewitness when I finally went to Berlin to meet Erica for the first time many years later.

Though the skeletal reduction of the city made it nearly impossible to find residents who had been there at the fall, Daddy had been able to locate Ilonka and Erica and gave them Mutti's address.

Daddy had gotten hold of a jeep and drove to the little village of Niedermarsberg near Frankfurt in Westphalia. It had been late in December 1938 when he last walked up the steep hill to his house to say good-bye to his family. Now, seven years later, he was standing in front of that very same house. The people who lived there vaguely remembered the name of Meyerhoff but claimed they had not the slightest notion of who had lived there before them or the tragic circumstances of their departure.

His father had been both rabbi and cantor for Marsberg. On the Sabbath, Christian townsfolk on their way past the synagogue dallied in the street to hear his magnificent voice. He died when Daddy was still a boy, long before Hitler came to power, which spared him the horror that was to follow. But what had become of Anna, his mother? What was the fate, my father wondered, of his two good and fine and handsome little brothers, Helmut and Ernst? Boys so bright, so happy, so full of life, as he described them to me years later. And what of his sister, Elizabeth? She had turned eighteen years old just as the war began, having blossomed into a lovely young woman. She was the only member of his family he was able to trace. Liesl had been sent in a transport to Danzig a scant year earlier, then was taken to nearby Stutthoff Concentration Camp where, at the Danzig Anatomical Medical Institute, Professors Spanner and Volman were experimenting on how best to render their victims into the commercial products of leather and soap. Her trail ended there.

Daddy went to his father's gravesite. It was littered with trash and overgrown with weeds, and the tombstones were askew, many fallen or pushed on their sides. He ordered the *Burgermeister* to appear and demanded that the Jewish cemetery be groomed at once. A labor force of old men, women, and girls was gathered together from the village. Not a young man or a boy was among them. Familiar faces among the citizenry avoided his eyes as they pulled up brambles and weeds and lifted tombstones to their right positions. One of the men was the father of a boy Daddy had grown up with, his best friend, Rudy. Daddy asked about him.

"Stalingrad," the man said. "Few of our sons came home," he added wryly, "but here you are."

At first, something about the tone of the remark disturbed Daddy, but he accepted it on face value as an expression of satisfaction that at least he had survived. Later, as he turned it over in his mind, it began to ring in his ears as an innuendo that the clever Jews, in true form, had once again somehow managed to manipulate the world and remain alive while good Christian Aryan German boys bled and died. Turning the truth upside down was a skill left over from the demised regime that had killed his son.

"Let us go to Germany, Mutti. I want to see my father."

"*Niemals!*" she shouted. "*Niemals!* Never, never will I ever set foot in Germany again."

She hadn't ever exploded at me in anger before. Benny told her it would be impossible to organize such a trip at that time, but it was reasonable for a child to want to see her father. Mutti said she couldn't go back, any more than he could, to a Germany that no longer existed, nor could Ma-ri-an-na "go back" to a country where she had never been and didn't belong.

It was then that I knew she saw Germany as a magnificent picture frame out of which an exquisite masterpiece had been torn, that I could never be everything in the world to her, for no matter how hard Mutti gazed into my eyes, what she sought was not to be found in me, but in the phantoms of her family, their three-dimensional personalities still acting out their lives in her heart and mind. But all of them were gone, vanished into the great graveyard that was Europe.

You must understand that Mutti had a keen sense of humor. She was the first to laugh at any joke. She was forthright and held her head high. Had you met her, you'd have been drawn to her by her compelling charm, delightful accent, and sunny disposition, which made it all the harder for her to mask her hopelessness, not from others but from me. Hopelessness because there was no "making good again." She was never going to get back what she was robbed of and found hard to live without. It never got better. She went about her life in a state of altered consciousness, loving, productive, but somehow unaware of herself, endlessly waiting, coasting, an equilibrium of opposing forces between now and death.

That night, Benny taught me a bedtime prayer:

Blessed be His Holy Name,
God lift the sun at break of day.
And if by deeds shall I be known,
Let good be reaped, where I have sown.

Later, when I was supposed to be asleep, I heard the adults talking.

"Shouting implants the tragedy deeper still in her and hobbles you, Lotte, if you clutch it so hard to yourself," emphasizing, as was his custom, his next word, "Orrr." He would pause until he had your full attention and only then continue. "Orrr, you can release the past and keep your eyes in front of you and never forget that tomorrow reflects the things you do and think today to bring it into being. Do you understand?"

Benny was a great believer that regardless of upbringing or tragedy, healing comes through the ideas we hold, and therefore we must guard with vigilance at all times the thoughts we choose to dwell on. The key is our internal dialogue, what we whisper to ourselves all day.

"Hating those who would harm you brings you down and concedes victory to them because it helps them to achieve their purpose. Hating is their game, and they have drawn you into playing it with them."

This was the central idea to healing he exhorted us to consider.

At breakfast the next morning, Benny burst into laughter when I said I was going to remind myself all day that I could make today a good yesterday to look back on tomorrow.

"You are a clever little girl. You have shown that the idea works backward and forward."

Mutti laughed, too. The perplexing subject of hate, forgiveness, and redemption has not changed since the beginning of time.

"*Dankeschön*, Rabbiner Gottschalk."

"You don't have to call me Rabbi Gottschalk," he said. "From now on, I am just Benny."

"Will you pick me up every day after school, Benny?"

"Of course, I will, Ma-ri-an-na."

The SS had allowed Benny to leave with nothing but a suitcase, which I still have. They took everything from him. But he was in our lives now and he would protect and care for us. I took the rabbi's hand. The old friend of my grandfather and my mother was now my friend.

47

*Rabbi Gottschalk, whom I knew as
just Benny, in Los Angeles, 1945.*

Christmas Eve came, and Benny renewed a family tradition. We took the bus downtown and bought a Christmas tree. We waited until the last possible moment because there are huge markdowns on Christmas Eve and we had hardly a penny to spare.

"Not too large and not too small. Just the right-size tree to take home with us on the bus."

"Why does a rabbi buy a Christmas tree?" I asked.

"To honor the memory of your grandfather."

"Der Alte Fritz?"

He began to laugh, as the tears that masquerade as merriment filled his eyes. People stared. Benny didn't care.

"Der Alte Fritz," he said at last. "I had almost forgotten. You must understand why to call him Der Alte makes me laugh. Because I will tell you, your grandfather was in mind and heart the youngest man I have ever known. There was much mischief making in that house,

My uncle, Mops, with the beloved Klarchen, 1930.

and he did his share. American slapstick comedy choked him with laughter. Which is not to say he wasn't strict. About the Christmas tree, to answer your question, I also must tell you about dear Klarchen."

"Who is Klarchen, Benny?"

"Klarchen was for many years the housekeeper of the Wachsners, but in truth, she was a much adored member of the family. Every year Der Alte Fritz brought home a Christmas tree to put in her room so she could celebrate this most joyous day of her faith in their Jewish home. Your grandfather came to me to discuss having a tree, so we examined the issue from all angles. On balance, from a religious point of view, we decided it might be the highest expression of his Jewish heart to salute the sacred day of a beloved Christian under the protection of his roof. When your mother was a girl, on Christmas Eve her friends came by with Christmas gifts, and they stayed to watch Klarchen light the candles."

"Erica? Ursula? Ilonka?"

"*Ja*, the girls. But Ilonka was already a woman. She had a splendid voice of her own. She taught your mother how to sing. Well, it was a beautiful thing to hear them sing their carols as they stood around the tree. Mops, too, delighted in the glow of the candles. We buy a tree today so that we may always celebrate how much it meant to Der Alte Fritz as a Jew to see to it that the tradition of Klarchen's religion not be denied her in his house. Lotte will be surprised by the tree. It will bring back memories that will make her happy."

Mutti said not a word when we came home with the tree. She took out the cloth bag of antique Christmas ornaments and little candle clips that had come in the carton of things from Berlin.

"My God," Benny gasped, "but these are Klarchen's. I remember them well."

Mutti knelt beside me and searched out my eyes. "Yes, these were Klarchen's. They are very old and were passed down in her family from generation to generation. Your grandfather could not bear to see such beautiful ornaments go unused. When Klarchen had to leave, she gave them to me. She asked me never to forget her. I never will. I thought I would never see them again. I know she would want my daughter to have them, and now, *Liebchen*, they are yours."

"How did they get in the package, Mutti?"

"I had to leave everything behind. All I could take was a suitcase."

"What happened to Klarchen?"

"I don't know."

Mutti showed me how to use the clips to mount the candles on the branches, and we began to decorate the tree. It is a beautiful thing to see antique ornaments and real candles glowing on a tree.

"Everything is now as it was," she said on Christmas Eve, "except to see Klarchen light the candles. Dear Klarchen told us her cousin, the flatterer who used to come often to our house, bowing and scraping, to pay us a visit, had joined the SS. She wanted us to know how ashamed of him she was."

I am touched in a special way by Klarchen's Christmas ornaments, I suppose because they seem out of context with the rest of the contents of the carton that came from Berlin. Yet the girls thought they were important enough to pack for the future remembrance they would provide of the values and kindness and sensitivity of my grandfather's home in the Berlin of those days. For that reason, they are very succinctly to the point. Somewhere along the way, Lotte or Benny told me that beloved Klarchen had to leave because the new laws said she must. When the Nazis took away the citizenship of Jews in 1935, Aryans were forbidden to work in their households.

"Klarchen cried when she left. We all cried. She left a big hole in our hearts when she was gone."

Benny's congregation grew as word spread among the German Jews who made Southern California their home. Some were elderly worshippers from Benny's former flock at the New Reform Synagogue in Berlin who longed to hear their very beautiful old German synagogue liturgy and to attend religious services conducted in German. Mutti and I began to attend his Friday night services. From the pulpit one Friday night I heard him say, "We extol the Godly side of ourselves and act out of it to improve the world. There are others who celebrate the cruelty to be found in the human heart, and they have gathered great strength from it. They think our way makes us weak and soft and sentimental. But, as has recently been shown, in the end, they have been destroyed."

Benny's sermons centered around ethics. He also had much to teach about how to hold ourselves in the face of tragedy, ever returning to the enigma of hate and forgiveness. At home, the message continued.

"It is not a choice to hate those who would destroy us, dear child, because to return their hate is to destroy ourselves. That would be helping them, wouldn't it?"

"Yes, Benny."

"So we forgive them, not for their sake alone, but most of all for our own. Do you understand?"

"No, Benny."

"Think of it this way. They chose to make us their victims and we were powerless. That was their choice, and we couldn't do much about it, could we?"

"No, we couldn't, Benny."

"Today, we have a choice, and we have the power to do something about it."

"What can we do, Benny?"

"We have the power to forgive them. Until we forgive them, we remain their victims, and why would we choose to do such a silly thing as that? Why would we choose to remain their victims?"

"We wouldn't, Benny."

"Then what must we do?"

"Forgive them."

"But," said Benny, "we must never forget."

Early one Sunday morning, a strange man's voice roused me from sleep.

"I followed a trail to Landsberger Allee," he said. "The building is just a pile of rubble. There was no trace of Mops. If he was still alive, he would have tried by now to contact you. You have to face it. No point in keeping your hopes up."

Mutti was standing over my bed, and beside her, larger than life, was the soldier in the picture, Daddy himself, Warren Meyerhoff. He was the conquering hero come home in the night from a war he had fought against German boys just like the ones who had been his friends at school in Niedermarsberg a few years earlier. Daddy smiled at me. I remember that very instant feeling for the first time protected, with not a thing in the world to worry about ever again. He picked me up and swung me around and did somersaults with me, and he hugged me and kissed me. Then he went to sleep for days.

"War does something to a man," Mutti said. "Paula thought the same when my father came home in the First World War."

Is it any wonder that a soldier's faith in the human race is shattered by the carnage all about him, of friends and enemies alike? And

My father, U.S. Army sergeant Warren Meyerhoff, 1944.

most of all because he is a part of it, a perpetrator like the rest, who is forced to find the killer in himself. This is why every soldier must believe he is on the right side.

I have two photographs of Daddy's mother, Anna, that came in the carton. I think I look like her. Mutti said Der Alte Fritz adored her. She had worked her fingers to the bone to give her children the education they deserved. She was a strict taskmaster who expected and got top academic performance from them. She had made Daddy practice his violin four hours a day and saved money to send him to Berlin to continue his education and to interview for the philharmonic. But it was too late. There was no chance of his landing an assignment at a time when Jewish musicians were being let go from every orchestra in Germany. He had met Lotte at university, and the pressure of the times threw them together. The Meyerhoffs had relatives in America who would sponsor them. The Wachsners could scrape together the few assets that remained to them to purchase the impossible: steamship tickets and landing permits for Havana. I don't know whether they would have been a match under normal circumstances, but in the intense atmosphere of the times, they became infatuated with each other. You can understand why both families gave them their blessings. Once in Cuba, they would somehow find a way to bring all of their family members over. Today, the plan seems vague and unrealistic, but they were not naive. My family clung to this belief because they had nothing better to hope for. Looking back, Mutti realized that Daddy was hardly more than a boy and not ready for such responsibilities. Our sponsor, Daddy's cousin, was the proprietor of a shoe store in a small town in Alabama, and he gave my father his first job.

"Just imagine a tall, gangly German boy with no English and no interest, trying to sell shoes to Southern ladies in a small town in the Deep South." Mutti said Daddy hadn't liked taking orders in German, and he demonstrated the same reluctance in English. She half grinned. It is thought to be a Jewish quality, an instrument of survival, to find humor in the most tragic of circumstances.

It wasn't long before we struck off again, moving around a lot with no sense of direction. Daddy called every motel a "pit stop on the way to somewhere else." When we reached Los Angeles, he enlisted in the army, and our breadwinner returned to Europe to fight back.

But the week he came home was magical. We had my father all to ourselves. I was the apple of his eye. I learned what it was to be held in the protective embrace of a loving father. But I learned better what a father's love is when it is withdrawn. That precious week would have to last me the rest of my life, for the next day the paternal half of my legacy as a child of survivors unfolded. The father I had yearned so long to meet so quickly said good-bye. He asked my mother for a divorce.

In Germany, his battalion had come upon a likely site to bivouac, an estate in Bad Wildungen not far from Marsberg. Daddy, as interpreter, was sent to inform the occupants that the army was going to take up residence. The handsome conqueror knocked on the door of the manor house and was greeted by a dazzling young blond beauty, the daughter of the estate. The family had sacrificed its only son, her seventeen-year-old brother, to Hitler's ambition for Deutschland Über Alles (Germany over all). I think I remember hearing that he, too, fell in Russia.

The magnetism was instant. Her family was appalled when she and my father fell in love, not so much because he was Jewish, but because he was married and had a wife and a daughter at home in America. Mutti consented to the divorce. She would not stay in a marriage in which she wasn't loved, nor would she obstruct his happiness. I couldn't understand why the love I thought my father had for me vanished so swiftly, or why receiving my love meant so little to him. When I was old enough to understand, my intellectual grasp did little to soothe me.

The young woman's parents threatened to disinherit her, but Daddy brought her home to America and married her. Her parents relented only when she announced she was pregnant with their first grandchild. My father took her to meet Mutti, if you can imagine. She was truly the most beautiful woman I had ever seen. Mutti and she spoke the same cultured German and they became friends, until her pregnancy. After the first baby was born, I hardly saw them anymore, and my father, for the most part, put me out of his life. All of this makes me wonder whether there is truth in a theory of my grandfather's, that there is a strange dance among men, written in the genes, that beckons them in some primordial way to act out their mutual drama of destruction. Did my father wonder whether his new wife's brother had killed Jews in Russia before he himself was killed? He wasn't SS, just a foot soldier in the Wehrmacht, but the regular army was also in the thick of it, doing its murder and cruel deeds to protect the purity of German blood.

My father, Werner Moritz-Meyerhoff, 1918.

My paternal grandparents, Levi and Anna Meyerhoff, 1916.

My father and his violin.

The Meyerhoff family with Mops (far right) and a family friend, about 1937.

Elizabeth, Anna, Helmut, and Ernest Meyerhoff, 1939.

*Lotte on her wedding day,
1938.*

Lotte and Warren Meyerhoff, 1938.

During the war, no banner headlines in the Nazi newspapers of the Third Reich ever proclaimed to the public that the "Final Solution to the Jewish problem in Europe" was under way. There was no gloating in the official party newspaper, *Der Sturmer*. None of Herr Goebbels's grandiose radio pronouncements bragged to the German people that their fathers and sons and husbands in the Wehrmacht and the Einsatzgruppen were out slaughtering whole populations of Jews and other *Untermenschen* (less than human beings) in their path. The leadership was always sensitive to public sentiment as a test of how far the leaders could go in plain sight of the people, chipping away at them bit by bit until fear seized them completely. The irony of it all.

Such tragic recollections. Now, more of it was heaped on Mutti. She sat staring into space when I came home from school one day. What had happened? A letter had arrived from Germany announcing that Ilonka had died. I don't remember what caused her death, or from whom the notice came—more than likely Erica. Only that Lotte's grief came from some deep, unconsolable place in her that truly mourned. How wrong it was that fate made such friends live out their lives in separation. In that better world of Benny's, friends who love one another so deeply will never be made to part. Ilonka intrigued me. She was young and her death was unexpected. It has been a challenge to find out much about her. By the process of elimination I deduced that she risked the most for her friendship. How courageous she was, how magnificently and without fanfare she had played a dangerous game for her beliefs. It was a blessing that Benny was there to console Lotte. I didn't know what to do.

It must have been this news, on top of my father's defection, that pushed calm, metaphysical Benny's buttons. It was one of those rare times I saw him seethe with anger. He was furious with my father for having betrayed his trust. He remembered Paula's reservation that Warren was too immature, just a boy who hardly could have been expected to handle the responsibilities placed upon him by emigrating with a new wife to America. Moreover, as soon as they arrived, with no experience and no contacts, how could my father possibly have managed to find a way to get the entire family out of Germany?

Paula and Rabbi Gottschalk on my mother's wedding day, 1938.

This would have called for more diplomatic finesse than even a Henry Kissinger could muster.

But if my father was gone from my life, Benny was now a part of my new American family, and in him I found all of the qualities of a wonderful male role model. He had perfect recall when it came to the Wachsners of Berlin. So intimately had he lived out his years with them as clergyman, counselor, and friend, he thought of his own life as intertwined with theirs and thus was part of the family. From the things he told me during my growing-up years, I pieced together a family profile that went beyond what Lotte had long forgotten or possibly had ever known. Benny had officiated at every rite of passage, including the wedding of Lotte's parents in 1914, her birth and her mother's funeral in 1915, her father's second marriage to Paula in 1919, Ernst's birth in 1920, and her own wedding in 1938.

It went back even further than that. Benny told me how, in 1914, his synagogue and every German synagogue was filled to standing room only, to pray for Germany when Kaiser Wilhelm declared war and asked God for His blessing. The kaiser told the nation, "Today, I see before me only Germans." The Jews of Germany heard that loud and clear. It was certain confirmation from the mouth of their monarch that their constant, historic cycle of oppression and recuperation in the life of the Fatherland had finally brought them as full-fledged members into the German community. For the moment, all differences melted away. A sudden kinship appeared among the vast majority of Germans, a full-blown *völkisch Camaraderie* (the whole German people's comradeship) that could be felt in the heart. That brief time is still remembered as special in the life of the nation.

Fritz Wachsner had gotten his Ph.D. at Jena University a year before the war began and was one of the thousands who proudly presented himself to do his duty for his country. My grandfather and his bride to be, Charlotte Apolant, happened to attend Benny's synagogue on that historic day. They liked the rabbi and chose him to perform their wedding ceremony before my grandfather answered the call to arms.

Benny was there the day Mutti came into the world in the same moment her mother departed it. "Such a beautiful woman she was!" Benny said. "So young, so full of excitement and life, hardly out of her teens, so vibrant."

The army gave my grandfather leave to arrange for the care of the baby, and he entrusted her to an aging aunt, Tante Francia. His wife had been everything he wanted in a mate. They were granted so little time. It had been only two years earlier that my grandfather had asked for her hand in marriage. Among the documents that came in the carton, I found a letter from him to her parents, dated March 28, 1913, in which he listed his qualities as a proper candidate to be their son-in-law. He wrote, "Please subject me to the rigid standards worthy of a man who asks for your daughter's hand in marriage. I offer you and Lotte three things: I am a hard worker. I have a happy temperament which, even in the saddest moments, will come forth. And I have the urge to understand other people and bring them happiness. And I have never been in jail."

My maternal grandfather, Fritz Wachsner,
a soldier in the German army in World
War I, 1914.

My maternal grandmother, Charlotte, after
whom my mother was named, 1906.

*My grandfather with his fiancée,
Charlotte Apolant, 1914.*

*My grandmother Charlotte (center),
with her good friends Paula Pese (left)
and Trude Pese (right), 1910.*

It hurts me to think that in the end, his "happy temperament" was not enough to triumph over his "saddest moment," and my wonderful grandfather's death came not with respect and blessing for the kind life he lived, but with cruelty.

There was nothing Benny could do as a rabbi or a friend to console my grandfather for the loss of his wife—my grandmother—in childbirth. His whole purpose in life now focused on his new daughter, whom he named Charlotte after her mother. And, of course, it was Benny who officiated at the old tradition of the blessing and naming of the baby in the synagogue, as well as at my grandmother's funeral in Berlin's vast Weissensee Cemetery. Grieving beside the soldier was his wife's closest friend, Paula Pese, who assured him that she would look in on the baby while he was gone. Then my grandfather returned to active duty for the glory of the kaiser and Deutschland.

The war siphoned off the farmhands of Germany, leaving too few of them to milk the cows and harvest the crops. Even basic foodstuffs were scarce. As an infant, Mutti had no milk. With her mother dead and not a single available wet nurse to be found in Berlin, all Tante Francia had to feed her was tea. It had a lasting effect on her health.

All these things that Benny told me were not only of personal interest, for they were tied so closely to world events that led from the First to the Second World War, the defining events of the twentieth century which had so intimately affected my family. Spurred on by the need to fill in the gaps, I began to do my own reading of German history to put what Benny imparted to me into its historical setting.

By 1918, the bloody battlefields of France were at a stalemate between the Axis powers and the Allies. The trenches on both sides were filled with the dead and dying, the starving and weary, and neither side could claim victory on the field of battle. But time was on the side of the Allies. America had entered the war the previous year, providing an unending supply of everything the Allies needed to continue the war, while Germany had run out of food and raw materials and no longer could sustain hostilities.

My mother, Charlotte Wachsner, 1916.

My mother with Paula, who cared for Lotte after her mother died and later married my grandfather, 1919.

My grandfather Fritz with his students in Berlin at the Jewish "show" school set up by the Nazis in the early 1940s.

General Ludendorf of the German General Staff blinked first and asked for an immediate truce. Later, he showed himself to be a coward and a liar when, to deflect his own responsibility, he blamed the defeat on the Jews and invented the myth that they had "stabbed Germany in the back." The pope called for a "just and honorable peace." The kaiser abdicated the throne and fled to Holland, and the terrible war was over. But where was the "honorable peace"? This was supposed to be an armistice, a stand-down, a cessation of hostilities, a truce, not defeat. The outspokenly patriotic German public was not prepared, nor were my grandfather and his fellow soldiers ready to accept it, for they had not been defeated on the field of battle. The sense of betrayal that pervaded Germany became accepted truth, and, in the public mind, you know who was to blame.

Paula had indeed looked in on my mother, baby Charlotte, while my father was away at war, and she was there for him when he returned in dismay. She despaired with him for the future of their country without the monarchy.

Lotte cherished the story her father told her of that day in November 1918 when he came home from the war and saw her for the first time since her birth. He had just been mustered out of his unit, which itself was then disbanded under the terms of the Treaty of Versailles. Lotte's imagery was vivid, and I relived the excitement as if I had been there with them that day.

He knocked on the door and let himself in. His gloom darkened the room. His uniform was tattered and torn, his face grimy and unshaven. Baby Charlotte was three years old and had never seen him before, but she knew that there stood her father. Tanta Francia let out a shriek and rushed to him, and took the weary, disillusioned soldier into her embrace, the better to feel that all his limbs were still attached. His eyes focused on Lotte. She was dressed in a dirndl and had long braids and a great big red bow in her hair. A smile broke out on his face and the lights came on in her world. He instantly realized that having his daughter in his life meant the world to him. It reaffirmed that life was worth living after all. He said that just to see what a wonderful little girl she had become restored his faith in their postwar future. Little did he know. He picked her up and smothered her with *kusses*. She blushed and overflowed with pride and could hardly breathe. He hoisted her, squealing with laughter, onto his shoulders and danced her around the room. She looked down at him, the better to see her Vati's face. He lifted a brow to peek up at her. Their eyes met and there was mischief in hers. Beneath his swooping mustache and beard, he, too, was laughing, and the depression that had come through the door with him vanished. Mutti herself remembered only that his bearing was ramrod straight as if he were a general decked out with a hero's chest full of medals, and she saw her father that way ever after.

Fritz Wachsner's uniform was mended and cleaned so that he could don it one more time for a most solemn occasion. A great bronze Yahrzeit plaque was to be installed in Benny's New Reform Synagogue to honor the sixty-two members of his congregation who had fallen in battle for Deutschland.

Benny recalled the event with Teutonic pride. "Your grandfather wore his tunic that day and brought little Lotte with him to help us lay down a great wreath of flowers. White lilies for the purity of their sacrifice, red roses for the blood they shed for their country."

The government crumbled without a kaiser. Left and right were in open warfare; there was revolution in the streets. But when the chaos cleared, the great majority of Germans had chosen democracy. It was the clear will of the people. The other democracies of the world might have been expected to extend a helping hand to the fledgling government, but the Treaty of Versailles was designed to punish Germany as a sovereign nation. The Allies did all they could to put stumbling blocks in the path of the new Weimar Republic, and Germany was forced to sign the treaty as a nation beaten into submission. The alternative was occupation.

The sheer number of military dead was appalling. Sons never returned to the farms. The food shortage was acute. People went hungry while the Allies withheld the food supplies they had promised to the German people. Starvation played right into the hands of the newly formed Nazi Party and brought attention to Hitler, who called the signing of the treaty a national shame. He picked up on Ludendorf's slogan blaming the Jews for "stabbing Germany in the back," thereby discovering his oratory skills and the power of the lie to be his strongest gifts. It would take little more than a decade for him to come to power.

Lotte remembered herself as a child who also went hungry. "When my father came home, he moved us to a farming village where he could barter his teaching skills for food. He farmed in his spare time just to be sure we had enough to eat."

The economy rose and fell and rose again and Berlin, for a while, was swimming in prosperity. At some time in the early 1920s, Lotte didn't remember when, they returned to Berlin where Der Alte Fritz took up a teaching post. His reputation grew by leaps and bounds.

Lotte cupped my chin in her hand and caught my eye. "But he never thought in terms of his reputation, just his good name."

She held my gaze until it was clear to both of us that I could discern the difference.

"Your grandfather's classes were popular. Imagine his lecture hall as large as a theater filled to capacity. He liked so much to enter the hall just after the hour in his white laboratory smock. The class would fall silent. I think I intimidated him when he knew I was auditing his class because he didn't want me to see him as such an extrovert in public. But there were times he didn't know I was there, and he put on quite a show. He usually sat down at his desk and shuffled through his paperwork. Then he peered out at the class with surprise, as if he had forgotten his students were sitting there, waiting for class to begin. He got up and wandered around his desk, deep in thought, then leaned back against his laboratory table and kept silent, during which time each of his students was sure he had made eye contact with him or her alone. Only then did he begin his lecture, starting with a joke that shed light on his subject. Because Papa reasoned that when he engaged his students in laughter, he had their attention and his lectures would reach deeper into their intellect. The thing of it was, Der Alte Fritz subtly knew how to render clear the most difficult of subjects, for when the laughter died down, his class would discover that in the meanwhile an arcane point had lost its mystery. *Ja,* we could be out with students from any part of Berlin and hear some academic type mention Professor Wachsner. I admit I loved it. It made me so proud. Especially in front of my girlfriends. You don't know how crazy they were about him. Especially Ursula. *Ja,* Ma-ri-an-na, the things you ask of me I know too little and I know too much."

CHAPTER 4

Hands across the Holocaust

I WONDER HOW IT WOULD HAVE CHANGED THINGS had Mutti taken me to Germany when I was a child, as I wished. The names of the people she cried out in her sleep were important to me, too. I used to daydream of Der Alte Fritz putting me up on his shoulders and dancing me around the room the way he did with Mutti when he came home from war. It is easy to surmise that he is a professor by his Prussian bearing, his pince-nez glasses and mustache, and the gold watch chain with an academic key he wears across his vest. His hair is thinning. He exudes an odd mix of authority, discipline, and wisdom, and he has a kind and loving face. I discover how it feels to be protected. He is charming. With all of his dignity, there is nevertheless an edge of the prankster about him. When he laughs, it is uproarous. We have a heart connection.

In my dreams I also meet Mutti's little brother, my Onkel Ernst, "Mops," a brilliant student and a mischief-maker whom Mutti said I reminded her of because we have the same smile. I anoint him my favorite uncle.

And I am in the kitchen of Mutti's stepmother, Paula, who raised my mother from infancy as her own. Papa said that Paula's table was "better known among more people than a good restaurant needs to stay in business," but Mutti cannot enter the kitchen. She has always been first in all of her classes and must keep up her academic standing and bear down on training her voice. For me, though, Paula has relaxed this policy. She will teach me how to cook.

I sit beside Der Alte Fritz's mother, my great-grandmother Fanny. Her face is white and wrinkled as a prune. She is very old and very wise, and she has on a long black dress. I watch her deft fingers coif her silken silver hair with an antique brush and comb and hand mirror of ebony, ivory, and tortoise that she says will someday be mine. She peers out at me over her granny spectacles and in an instant sees all, knows all that I am. As I grow up, she will impart her wisdom to me. She, too, is my legacy.

Would going to Germany when I was a child have rid me of my fantasies about a family I could never meet? And how would it have been if the Four Girls from Berlin had met again? Would they have fallen right back into, or even come near to, the old closeness of the girlhood they shared? The awful disaster they lived through and witnessed from both sides must have sent all their lives awry.

Lotte got sick when I was thirteen. She suffered three major surgeries that year and was bedridden two years more, during which I had to call for ambulances, sometimes in the middle of the night. We lived close to school, so I was able to walk home at lunchtime every day and make sure that she ate. After school, I got right back home again to take up my duties. In the middle of all this, Benny's health began to fail and I became a caregiver twice over. I felt like a grownup, to be needed and depended upon. Lotte never stopped telling me how able I was and how much my taking care of them meant to her. Who else if not me?

Mutti's health improved, but resuming her tough schedule of nursing was out of the question. I lied about my age and got a job at Bullocks Wilshire. A highlight of my teen years was to buy Lotte an upright piano. It was criminal for her not to at least have a piano to play when she could no longer sing.

72

I studied, worked hard, and had goals, and I charged toward them in the best American entrepreneurial spirit, marveling at the persistence it took for Jews through the millennia to do the same successfully when the odds were stacked so very much against them, when time and again, history put them on a path to a dire fate not of their making, which was sealed before they were born, with nothing they could do to change it. Where did they get the courage to take responsibility for themselves when all they could do was stand by like mourners at their own funeral? Now the pattern had so recently repeated itself, but with all the tools of modern technology at the disposal of the murderers.

As I became a young woman, my interest in Germany, where so much of my family's history had played itself out, had not diminished. A sensation nagged me. Hitler had torn me out of my natural future. I knew all along that if I were ever to put the German claim upon my identity to rest, I had to break out and try to retrace Lotte's steps, to catch a glimmer, no matter how remote, of what her world was like. I tried to imagine the affront to her very core that she endured as girl becoming a woman in Nazi Berlin. If I could understand this, it might show me how to step back just long enough and far enough to stop seeing the world through her prism alone and find my own way. I would have to go away from her to come closer.

More than a destination on a map, Germany was an idea that seesawed between a heartfelt cultural connection and a heart broken by the betrayal of its own humanity. Would I go there in search of my German roots or to connect with my Jewish roots? Or were both bound together in the unique identity of the two-thousand-year-old German-Jewish experience, an interlacing the Nazis tried to untie and, in so doing, created instead the appalling history that will forever connect Jews and Germany?

I was twenty-two years old when I first went to Germany. All my life I had wanted to meet Lotte's old friends. If I could understand their handclasp so strong that years later not even the Holocaust had torn it apart, if I could catch but a glimpse from Ursula and Erica of

Mutti as a girl growing up in Nazi Berlin, and of her family, it might help to connect me to the life that would have been mine.

"Then go if you must," Lotte said. "You are old enough now to do as you please." Her melancholy at the very idea of my standing on the soil of her homeland betrayed her own impossible yearning.

Mutti wrote to tell them I was coming. Erica's reply said it was about time. She called me a branch missing from her own tree and said that meeting me would be more like a reunion. When Lotte read her letter, a grin blossomed on her face that offered a glimpse of the Berliner whose outlook was once so happy. Erica would add another tint to my portrait of Lotte, and she would retrace with me old steps the girls took in the days when their secret was to call themselves the Four Girls from Berlin. She would show me the town, a walk in the Grünewald, an outing at Wansee, a trip to Potsdam.

Ursula's answer took it for granted that I would stay with the Namgalies in Mölln in Schleswig Holstein where Bruno had long been the minister of the local Lutheran church. She said there was plenty of local color to interest me. Did we know that Til Eulenspiegel was buried in Mölln? There is a statue of the mischievous little imp in the town square. Legend says that if you rub his toe, all of your dreams will come true. My mother's friends looked forward to embracing me as their own. It was out of the question that I stay anywhere else. They would have it no other way.

I can only imagine what Ilonka would have had to say about Lotte and my grandfather. Ilonka had become more ambitious, even more so than he, for the career of her protégée. When that was destroyed and Lotte had to flee for her life, Ilonka transferred her devotion to the Wachsners and risked all to stay loyal to them until the end. Imagine the cat-and-mouse game she had played for a protracted period under the Nazis' noses. Mutti said she thought that malnutrition and a broken heart had cut Ilonka's life short after the war.

I wanted to create, in my mind's eye, a holographic image of my grandfather. It wasn't enough to know they called him Der Alte Fritz, Old Man Fritz, that he played the flute beautifully, or that he was a professor of biology and chemistry, loved by his students, esteemed by his colleagues, or that his hobby was rare stamps, of which he had assembled a major collection. I could never know enough about him, short of knowing him. Ursula could tell me the most. He had been Ursula's mentor. She truly adored him.

On my flight to Germany I began to feel sick. My strength ebbed. This was no time to be sick. I was on my way to the event of my life, meeting Mutti's friends, icons of my youth, Der Vier Berlinerinen. When we landed, I went to an airport pharmacy and asked the druggist to recommend something. When he replied in German, only then did I realize that I had slipped back seamlessly into the language of my childhood. As I went on to Mölln, I grew weaker and still refused to acknowledge it. I would brave it out. I arrived there at dusk and found the address. Hardly had I knocked when a women, blond hair streaked with gray, came to the door, and there, standing at the threshold, in a moment out of time, was Ursula herself.

"Ma-ri-an-na." Her smile began to quaver. She hid it with her hand. Her eyes were wet.

"*Endlich*," she said. "At last, you are here."

"*Ich bin so froh hier zu sein*, I'm so happy to be here," I replied.

"So! You speak German," she said in perfect English.

"*Ein bisschen*, a little."

"Your mother has taught you well."

"When I was small. I'm rusty now."

Lotte had told me long ago that Ursula was not very demonstrative of her emotions, but she was hugging me like someone who had loved me and lost me, then found me again.

"You don't look at all like your mother."

Just then, a stocky, balding man with eyeglasses poked his head through the door. He was just as I imagined he would be.

"Hello, Bruno," I said.

"*Mein Gott*. Ma-ri-an-na." His eyes opened wide. "You look just like your mother."

"*Nein*, there is no resemblance at all," came Ursula's definitive ruling on the matter. Bruno ignored it just the same, scrutinizing me with all the merriment of the mischief-maker in his eyes. I thought that if he stared any harder, he would surely find Lotte, the one he was looking for, hiding someplace not too deep inside me.

"But," he protested, appealing to reason, "she has the same smile. It runs in the family."

"*Ach so*, Ma-ri-an-na, he is right. You have the Wachsner smile. Lotte's *Tochter*, here! So many years. *Mein Gott*, Bruno. Can you believe it?"

He was shaking his head. "*Nein.* I cannot."

Twenty years had passed since the end of the war, and here I was with Ursula and Bruno, wanting to connect with them, hoping through them to reconnect in some way to the leitmotif of my life, the roots Mutti had left behind in 1939.

If you have never been greeted as a long-lost niece by a German *Tante* and *Onkel*, you will be hard-pressed to understand what it meant to me when Ursula and Bruno swept me into their home as family and left no doubt that I was the daughter of a mother who never stopped belonging to them.

"Come inside, Ma-ri-an-na." Ursula took my hand and led me through the door into the light. "And bring her bags," she demanded, calling out to goodnatured Bruno who had already scooped them up and was on his way inside with them. Adorning the walls were many African objects of great beauty that they had collected in Tanganyika. My eyes were drawn to a wedding portrait of a striking young couple. It was Jochen and his new wife, Rena. So this was what the little boy in the picture grew up to look like.

"You must tell us all about your mother," Bruno said. "*So eine wunderbare Stimme.* Oh, such a wonderful voice."

"And here you can speak English," Ursula said.

"We learned to speak English in Tanganyika," Bruno explained. "With you, we will practice our English."

"Mother remembers when you left for Africa. You had a classmate who went with you, Herbert Bahr."

"Oh, so she told you of Herbert." His eyes caught Ursula's.

"Mother wanted to go, too, you know."

"*Ja*, a long story," Bruno said. "A long time ago. Herbert is my best friend, still. His congregation is in Capetown. He writes and asks, 'What do we hear from Lotte?' Lotte writes and asks, 'What do we hear from Herbert?' We have given them news back and forth for years. I will write and tell him you are in Germany. He will be happy to hear about Lotte's daughter."

I came to learn that cooking was not one of Ursula's favorite pastimes, but for "Lotte's daughter," she had supper waiting.

"You must be hungry."

But I couldn't lift a spoon. The very thought of food made matters worse. I could no longer pretend. I was sick. The room began to spin.

Bruno peered at me over his glasses. Ursula stared hard at me under the light. She spoke, and there was alarm in her voice.

"She is tired now. We have plenty of time to talk." She drew Bruno aside and I could hear an urgent whisper.

"*Gelbsucht! Sie zieht nicht gut aus. Ihre Haut ist gelb, und die Augen!*"

Although my German is better than I think, it is not as good as I would like. They used the word *Gelbsucht*, which I had not heard before. They said they recognized my symptoms and that it was serious.

"Do not be afraid," Ursula said. "It is common in Africa. We must get you to hospital. Come. In Tanganyika we often saw this. We waste no time."

It was morning when I heard a doctor tell them they had saved my life and had they waited a few hours more, I most surely would have died. I was in and out of consciousness for weeks afterward. Images played like a loop in my delirium: I was aboard a great ship that sailed endlessly back and forth across the sea and was welcome at no port of call. "Outcast, you do not belong here. Go back where you came from." To the grave German soil from which I sprang, I must say, "*Grüss Gott*, hello again." I was in and out of this revolving circle, stuck full of tubes and IVs.

"*Gelbsucht*," the doctor said. "A most serious case of hepatitis. We must watch carefully until you are out of danger. You must rest.

We must build you up. It will take time." During my illness, my weight fell to ninety pounds. I had weighed one fifteen. It was to be three months before I could leave the hospital, a long period of waves of nausea, hyperventilating, and delirium to lie there and ponder whether the emotional nexus of coming to Germany had unbalanced my immune system.

A day hardly passed that Ursula or Bruno didn't sit by my bed while I was in and out of consciousness. Lotte called them every day. They calmed her and told her not to worry, that my doctors were the best. Calls came from Erica, too.

In the bed across from me was an amiable old woman with sparkling eyes and a vivacious personality that belied her advanced age. She was starving for companionship and grateful for a new patient with whom to share the time. No sooner had the doctor left when she roused me from my misery and talked to me.

"The doctor speaks English to you," she exclaimed with surprise. "But I was sure you were a German."

"I'm an American. Why did you think I'm German?"

"Often, I cannot sleep and am awake all night. I could not help but hear you speak German in your sleep."

This fascinated me. I never thought in terms of the language one dreams in. And why in German if I think in English? Perhaps because I had heard only German as an infant.

"What did I say in my sleep?" I asked the old woman.

"I could only make out '*Grüss Gott*,'" she said.

"*Grüss Gott*"? Where in the world had I picked up this expression? I asked Ursula what it meant in the vernacular. She said it is a term used more in southern Germany, perhaps mostly among the majority of Catholics who live there. "Greetings to God" is a lovely thing to say, just the sort of polite, impersonal greeting one might offer a stranger in Bavaria, for example, upon entering or leaving a shop. I learned from Lotte to use "*Tschuss*" or "*Wiedersehen*," as they do in Berlin.

"*Grüss Gott* is used for both hello and good-bye," the old woman further explained.

It seemed like an expression more apt for the Jews of Germany.

One day the radiant young man and woman in the wedding picture were standing at my door. They held between them a bouquet of flowers of every color.

"You must be Ma-ri-an-na," the woman said in perfect English, and with the most gracious of smiles, "I'm Rena."

"And I am Jochen Namgalies," he said.

They came closer and I saw that what they held was not a bouquet but a big bowl of different-colored sorbets arranged to look like flowers. The nurse followed them in and said the sorbet was too pretty not to let me see, but they mustn't stay long.

The old woman showed herself to be considerate and buried her head in a magazine to give us privacy. But I could see she found it harder to ignore the sorbet, so I said I could see no reason why they should not all polish it off together before it melted. This made her happy. She had found a new friend in me.

Rena and Jochen were still newlyweds. They had moved to Kiel, more than an hour and a half drive north from Mölln, to set up household. Both were teaching school.

"So you are the little girl whose picture came at the end of the war in a package of food from America," Jochen said. "I was only five or six, but I will never forget the packages that came, one after another. It was fantastic."

"We got a baby picture of you first, with your mother holding you in her arms," I replied. "It came in a carton of things from Berlin right after the war. We still have that picture."

Jochen remembered so vividly the packages Mutti sent the Namgalies family because they contained vital food, the difference between sustenance and malnutrition, perhaps even survival and starvation, a boon at the end of the war when Germans had not a morsel to eat.

"That was the first time I heard them speak of 'Lotte in America,'" Jochen said. "For a time, your mother was one of the few people they talked about from the past. They still don't like to talk very much about those days."

"Same with me. My mother doesn't like to talk about it, either. I didn't know a thing about her past until we got the carton from Berlin. That's when I first heard your parents' names, Bruno and Ursula. And Erica Poch and Ilonka Von Patti."

"Erica Poch. I know that name," Jochen said. "She is an old friend of my mother's from Berlin. I remember she came once to visit us in Mölln. But who is Ilonka Von Patti?"

"Ilonka died right after the war. That's probably why you don't know of her. I don't know much about her myself. *Aber die vier waren enge Freundinen.* But the four of them were the dearest of friends. It was very special."

The nurse came and tapped her watch. I remember my disappointment that she was curtailing their visit so soon. I felt that their visit was not just a good deed to cheer the sick. I was drawn to them. There was something special about them, something that made me want to know them, feeling at the same time that I had known them all my life. Their smiles were not just the polite and sincere but donned smiles usually offered when meeting someone for the first time. Theirs shone from inside. When they said good-bye, I knew something very special had happened. The years to come would reveal the truth of this.

Ursula never missed a day to visit me during the months of my convalescence. I thanked her for the visit of Rena and Jochen.

"But I said to Jochen only that Lotte's daughter was in the hospital here in Mölln," she explained. "They came on their own."

Ursula always brought flowers, not for me alone, but for the old woman who thanked her to no end for being so kind and considerate.

Art was Ursula's passion. She aspired to reinvent herself as the successful painter of her teenage dreams. One day she brought a linocut she had made of the skyline of Mölln. In the foreground, boats drift on the lake and trees frame the roofs of the village. At the center is the church with its steeple pointing to heaven.

"This is for you," she said modestly of her picture, but her pride was hardly concealed from me. Feigning nonchalance, she began arranging the flowers by our bedsides so as to busy herself while I stud-

The linocut of Mölln that Ursula brought to me while I was recovering from hepatitis.

ied it, though I saw how eagerly she awaited my reaction. It touched me how much my approval of her picture meant to her. Its strength came to me in its understatement, a disarming quietude as simple and lovely as a haiku. No facile reach for effect, just a few deft cuts, printed in black and sepia, that create an inner stillness. It made her so happy that I was pleased to have it.

"Besides, you will hang it in your home in America. Lotte has never seen my work."

Ursula told me about the years she had spent with Bruno as the wife of a missionary in Africa. How very much she loved and missed the indigenous people among whom they worked tirelessly. She greatly admired their art and the intrinsic beauty of the simple objects of their daily use. She and Bruno had brought home to Germany a collection of native art, which made a visit to their house a special treat for me. Ursula loved Africa.

81

She hated talking about Nazi Germany. There were moments when I felt the full weight of all that had happened rise close to the surface between us, yet remain unspoken. I recognized the same familiar reluctance to revisit the Hitler years that I had with Mutti. Still, the missing years of their friendship grieved Ursula. Now I was in Mölln and her chance to get answers of her own overpowered her distaste for talking about it. She gave me my opening.

"We would not have thought such a thing possible when your mother and I were girls, to lose so many years. Since the war ended we have written to each other and still only write of what happens now in our lives. We never talk about . . ." Ursula floundered on finishing her sentence. "About Dr. Wachsner. I did not want to ask. I did not want to hear. It is a habit for us never to talk of these things."

I told her what she surely must have surmised, that my whole family had disappeared in the camps, and that Lotte was just as reluctant to tell me about it as Jochen said she and Bruno were to discuss it with him. It gave me my lead-in to ask what she remembered about my grandfather.

"He was the kindest and dearest man I have ever known. I always wanted to be at Lotte's house. It was a happy place to be. Your grandfather was closer to me than my own father. What a flautist the professor was! He had his own chamber music trio and gave concerts at home once a week. Music, music, music. Everybody came to Lotte's house in those days, even Party members."

I asked for her firsthand account of what he looked like. She threw back her shoulders like a soldier.

"Chin in and shoulders back," she said. "Very serious on the outside. Inside he was as funny as the children." She fell silent as she tucked my blankets around me. After a while, she continued. "To this day, your mother and I are very bad cooks because of him."

"Why?"

"Once you tasted Paula's cooking, you knew you couldn't reach such heights and you stopped trying. I didn't even let myself fry an egg anymore. But Dr. Wachsner wouldn't let Lotte go near the kitchen. He put his foot down. She didn't need to spend her time learning to

Grandfather Fritz the flautist with a trio, about 1908.

cook, he said, even from such a talent as Paula. Lotte was going to be a great singer."

"Mutti said they called him 'Der Alte Fritz.'"

"Der Alte Fritz." She laughed. "He would come home from school with his head swimming in theories and equations, and Lotte and Ernst would call him Der Alte Fritz just to get him started." Ursula's voice quivered, and her words began to spurt from her like water from a faucet. "Lotte's brother, Ernst, was a very naughty boy. He liked to play practical jokes on the professor. He would do anything to 'get his goat.' 'I told you not to call me "Der Alte Fritz," the professor roared. But he had his own sense of humor and called the boy 'Mops' instead of Ernst, his given name, to get even and told him what he was going to do to him when he caught him. I couldn't imagine such a dignified professor chasing his little boy around the house. And everyone was laughing, and then your mother opened her mouth and demanded the professor not to lay a hand on Mops, which was very brazen and very funny all at once, because your grandfather, after all, was as strict an authority as a German father could be. But he finally caught Mops anyway and tickled him until their sides ached with laughter. When they finally settled down, they didn't even have a chance to catch their breath. Lotte followed up on her own with a perfectly timed, 'Der Alte Fritz.' And Mops was bursting out laughing all over again, your grandfather, too, and he chased Lotte all over the house and everyone was bantering back and forth and laughing. It was not so much fun in my house. And Paula came out from the kitchen and called to everybody, 'Dinner is ready now. Come and eat now and stop having a good time.' The Wachsners were always open for a hearty laugh."

"What about Paula? Mutti always told me what a fabulous cook she was."

"Everybody loved your grandmother, Frau Wachsner."

"My stepgrandmother."

"*Ja*, but the only mother your mother ever knew. So mild. I never heard a harsh word. So kind, so gentle. Lotte could not have loved her birth mother more. If ever it was true that 'a woman's place is in the kitchen,' Frau Wachsner set the example, because her kitchen was her atelier, with herself as artiste in residence. She was La Chef Fantastique. 'Did you have enough, Ursula? Eat, eat.' No one ever turned down an invitation for Paula's cooking. She could have opened a restaurant.

"Erica and I went to a reception at Lotte's house for some of the musicians when the New York Philharmonic came to Berlin. Of course, Ilonka was always there. I think it was 1932. You never knew when a famous musician or physicist or clergyman or someone from the theater might be sitting at your elbow, or a hungry student with nowhere to go whom your grandfather dragged home for a hot meal. That is how your mother met your father. Well, that is what made a happy home, and that is what made the professor happy. Good discussions, a good dinner with interesting guests, and a fine wine. And for dessert? Paula's cakes and pastries. And after dinner, music. A lot of music. The family meant everything to him. I ought to know. He treated me like another daughter. Most of all, I remember his wise counsel.

Mops and Lotte, 1923. *Lotte and Mops, 1933.*

People coming and going all the time, seeking the professor's advice. Everybody looked up to him. He meant very much to me. I am glad I finally get it now off my chest. I wanted to for years, with no one to tell it to." She shook her head. "Your grandfather was a man to be proud of." She fussed again with my blanket and puffed up my pillow.

"What was my mother like in those days?"

Ursula pulled her chair closer. She had a way of tilting her head and bending to you to underline her words. "We were fifteen when I first met Lotte at school. She was just starting to train her voice then with Ilonka. She was always the best in all of her classes. There was no keeping up with her. We had a competition at school to write an essay on a subject of our own choice. The faculty was so impressed with Lotte's, they asked her to read her paper before the whole student body, despite the fact, you must understand, that the faculty and students alike were riddled by then with Party members. But scholastics came easily to her and she didn't have to work hard at it. Of course, with the professor for a father, you could hardly expect less. Only for the voice did she really push herself. Everyone took it for granted that she would be a great success. Oh, if only we could hear Lotte sing again."

"Everybody would like to hear her sing again," I said. "But she hardly sings anymore." It was 1930 when Mutti and Ursula turned

Paula was Le Chef Fantastique,
1935.

fifteen. That year, the Great Depression came to Germany. Hitler had worked the political convulsions of the country to his advantage by doing everything he could to add to the turmoil while claiming only he had the power to restore order. Now he could also use poverty, the breeding ground of tyrants. But for a while longer, it was still the Weimar Republic, and democratic constitution guaranteed the rights of all citizens.

"Just before we went to Tanganyika, your grandfather took us to Lotte's debut. If you could have seen her then, Ma-ri-an-na. She always claimed I was the pretty one, but she turned plenty of heads, though I don't think she paid attention. In an inner way, perhaps she didn't. And such eyes. I thought she looked just as an opera star should. No one ever heard a voice like hers. The voice of an angel. A diva in the making. We left Germany then. It was many years before the war began. I never thought I would not see the Wachsners again. We would have remained in Africa, but the British rounded up all the Germans and put

86

us behind barbed wire. That is where Jochen was born. They held us there until they could send us back to Germany in a prisoner exchange."

The direction her conversation had taken gave me the nerve to put a question to her that was hard for me to ask. Had she ever witnessed an anti-Semitic incident between Lotte and the Nazis? What came to mind was not a confrontation but a radio broadcast she had heard at Lotte's house soon after they met in 1930. It was a speech Hitler gave to the students of Germany. She remembered how embarrassed she was in front of the Wachsners. The Nazis had won almost half of the 110 seats of the Student Associations of Bavarian Universities and Colleges. It was just the kind of encouragement Hitler needed to measure public opinion for his plans.

"Hitler said if there was one thing that let him believe in a Nazi victory, it was the advance made by the Party among the students. Your mother was shocked. We were disillusioned. We, too, were German students. Professor Wachsner was outraged. My cheeks burned. I was ashamed in front of them. But the truth is that anybody is susceptible to these types of lies and rantings. Dr. Wachsner said not to worry, that students have always been headstrong and known to go too far. There were Nazis in his classes. One of them was his best student. But he pointed out that if almost half of the students voted for Hitler, more than half of them did not. Hitler was a symptom of the times."

I needed to know more and went deeper into my own reading of the history of those days. Germans were unemployed and desperate. Violence was growing in the streets. Hitler misdirected their anger by blaming the Jews for Germany's problems, and although he never earned a majority of the vote, millions flocked to his call. It was *Gleichschaltung* in action, the familiar conditioned reflex of lockstep conformity out of the German past. This, I learned, was the frightening climate in which Mutti and her girlfriends had grown to young womanhood.

My grandfather was, as his father before him had been, a stubborn patriot. It was the Teutonic side of his nature, his stiff-backed German honor, not his stiff-necked Mosaic ethics, which made the prospect of becoming an outcast in his own homeland impossible for him to so much as contemplate. As conditions worsened, Mutti had to endure family lectures in defense of Germany, all their country's considerable achievements in the arts and science and how Germany won more Nobel Prizes than any other country on earth and was the first in the world to introduce compulsory public education for children. The professor wasn't aware of this, but when he lectured at home to the family, Mutti knew it was because of his own doubts and insecurities.

The political parties of Weimar were divided and indecisive and unable to act. Time was running out. The impasse could be broken only by bringing the Nazi Party into a coalition. This could not happen unless Hitler's demand to be placed at the head of government was met. Many rationalized that his anti-Semitism and the extremism in *Mein Kampf* were mere posturing, that his speeches were rhetoric propaganda designed to roil the emotions of the people and enroll new members. Coalition parties were sure they could control him once he was in office. On the fateful day of January 30, 1933, Hitler became the chancellor of Germany, and the end came swiftly to the Weimar Republic. It was the beginning of the descent into hell.

As a Jew, Mutti tried to ignore the daily barrage of slurs against the Jews and kept that "low profile." As a German, she could not. The disparagement of Jews as Germans tore her apart. Her soul belonged to *Judentum*, Judaism, but her heart was rooted in *Deutschtum*, Germanness. She was her father's daughter. She saw no conflict between the two.

I asked Ursula whether she remembered the time they were shopping when a parade of Hitler Youth came by, and a boy carrying a flag saw her and tripped into the fellow in front of him. The story made her laugh.

"What has your mother told you? It was her he was staring at."

"She said it was you."

"We wanted to laugh, but we dared not."

I told her how much it meant to Mutti when the carton came from Ilonka and Erica and her after the war, with all the Wachsner family things, and that we still had that picture of her in Tanganyika holding Jochen when he was born. She thought for a while.

"I don't remember," she said. "It is so long ago. But I will never forget the cartons of food that Lotte sent us. I don't know what we would have done without it. It saved our lives. We hadn't had sugar since we left Africa. And there were boxes of chocolate pudding. I didn't know the box already had sugar mixed in." She began to laugh. "American packaging was very strange to us then, so I put more sugar in with the pudding mix. It was so sweet, we could hardly eat it, but we ate it anyway and were glad to have it." Her laugh faded away and an utter sadness darkened her eyes, followed by a long uncomfortable silence.

"Dear Professor Wachsner. Such a man as that. They should have gotten out when they could. What use is there to talk about these things now?"

"They must be remembered."

"Maybe it is better to forget."

"The ones who did it would like to forget. They'd remember quick enough if it had happened to them. It's not so easy for the rest of us. I try to imagine how it would feel if something like that happened to me with the Nazis."

"*Ja*, there were confrontations. More than just a few. Lotte did not take to them very well. Ilonka once took us all to a very expensive restaurant. Kempinski's. It might have been someone's birthday; I don't remember. There was a table with Nazis. They were saying things. Well, you know, we were embarrassed. We knew the outrage your mother was feeling. I, too, was angry inside for her. And Ilonka was seething, but she tried to cool us all down. Erica would not be controlled. She simply would not stand for it. She got up and went over to one of them and dumped his hot soup in his lap. Yes. This was funny. We laughed. Even people at other tables were laughing. Ah, Ma-ri-an-na, what is the use?"

"I don't know. What about Herbert Bahr?"

"What did Lotte tell you? What do you know?"

"When I was seventeen, I had a crush on a boy. I didn't think I would ever get over it when he moved away. Mutti tried to console me. She said she understood because her heart had been broken when she was around my age, when her first love, Herbert Bahr, left Germany

89

and moved to Africa. He was Bruno's best friend, and all four of you were supposed to go to Africa together."

"Lotte and Herbert. I was there when they met."

You can well imagine, I was all ears.

"We Germans," Ursula continued, "had a tradition called *Vogelsang*. In those days, we loved to get together and go out all day and sing folksongs. It is not the tradition so much anymore. You would be surprised how many of us met those days in groups. There were bicycle clubs and hiking clubs, and we would go to the lakes around Berlin and old castles and ruins. You never had to go too far to enjoy a day out in the fresh air. But wherever we went, on the way we sang, and when we got there we sang.

"That day, Bruno and Lotte and Erica and I were on an outing to Wansee with our hiking group. We were all to meet at Charlottenberg Bahnhof and take the early train to Potsdam. Bruno invited a friend from the seminary. It didn't look as if he would make it, but at the very last moment before the train left the station, a tall, handsome fellow jumped on and took a seat across from your mother. This was Herbert Bahr. Bruno introduced him to Lotte and me. He hardly noticed us.

"He started to tune his guitar and idly began strumming a song, the 'Andante Moderato' from Brahms's *Fourth Symphony*. Such a beautiful melody. It happened to be one of Lotte's favorites. She began to hum along. You just couldn't believe how beautiful this was. She got out her lute and they played together, and then Herbert's wonderful tenor voice joined hers. All attention was on them. I think that is when he really noticed Lotte for the first time. Bruno was the next to add his basso in counterpoint, followed by the rest of us. It was quite a performance. It cast a spell over us. We earned a round of applause from the passengers, but Herbert's eyes hardly wandered from Lotte.

"When the train stopped in Potsdam, he took your mother's arm and helped her down from the carriage. Then we boarded the bus to Caputh. By the time we reached the lake, the two of them were off by themselves, chatting away, completely oblivious of the rest of us. Their love was not to be fulfilled in marriage, but in a lifetime of caring. After all these years, their letters always ask us to send their regards to the other. Herbert has been happily married for many years, but I think both of them still from time to time have thoughts of what could have been."

"Why couldn't it have been?"

"To answer this, it is better if you will ask your mother."

"Ursula, you said you would have stayed in Africa if not for the war."

"Yes."

"Why didn't the English round up Herbert and send him home, too? Why did they let him stay in Africa?"

Ursula shrugged her shoulders.

There was an unexpected and disheartening end to my stay in the hospital. During the three months I was there, as my symptoms abated, my roommate and I built a rapport. We talked about many things to pass the time. I admired the sparkle of this aged and wise woman. I am sure that I could not have been mistaken about our mutual good feelings. Yet from the day when Ursula and I had our heart-to-heart conversation until the end of my stay, something happened that caused me never to forget her and made me reflect on the unpleasant fact that charm, education, and culture and ignorance, narrowmindedness, and prejudice can all coexist in the same person.

That day, when Ursula said good-bye to her, the old woman, who could not have helped but hear us talk of the fondest moments and deepest anguish of our hearts, turned her back on Ursula. Ursula discerned this but pretended not to. I tried to make eye contact with the old woman. She averted her gaze. The smile she'd always had for me was gone. I was embarrassed. Once again, why should I have been the one to feel ashamed? Why did I fall in step with her narrowness and say nothing as if it were better to keep silent than talk of the horror? Was it for my sake or for the benefit of others like her who don't want to hear about it anymore? Or who possibly never wanted to hear about it in the first place? I notice discomfort come over some people when the subject comes up. It shames us to have our own contempt for ourselves thrown in our faces. Who wants to know this?

91

The ghosts crying out to be remembered, whose lives were snatched from them, want us to know this. They are not silent, old woman. If you had been one of them, Heaven forbid, you, too, would not want to be once forgotten and twice killed, your life as meaningless as that of an unnoticed ant on the sidewalk that someone steps on.

The old woman never uttered another word, paying just enough attention to stare at me with contempt, as if now that she had over-heard my background, she considered me as having falsely presented myself to her as a human being rather than as a Jew. In the morning, my vase of flowers still stood on the table by my bed where Ursula had left it. Hers was gone. Where had the woman's wisdom fled? How can ignorance be overcome with reason? Hatred with love? The big-ots want to hang on to their bigotry. They won't listen, and they are the ones who need to hear it. The ones who listen do so because they already understand. The day I left, I said good-bye. The woman ig-nored me. What was I to think? I came to Germany to understand. To do that, I thought I had to grasp the mindless hatred that cost my family and millions of innocents their lives. A tall order. And now, in this day and age, I had come face-to-face with only a small example of anti-Semitism in Germany and still I will never understand it. Of course, I tried to apply Benny's hard lessons.

"The Wachsners meant so very much to me," Ursula said loudly. You would have had to hear the heart connection in her voice, ex-pressed, so I thought, purposefully for the benefit of the old hypocrite.

Ursula sighed and clutched my hand in hers. It was heartfelt and reassuring and I fell asleep with Ursula holding my hand. I was released from the hospital a few days later on the condition that I not travel. I had to convalesce in Mölln for three months more. I spent them with Bruno and Ursula in their home, and there was, as Ursula said, "plenty of time" to sort things out. They doted upon me and looked after my every need. My strength returned. I gained weight and began to feel better than my old self.

On my first Sunday out, Jochen and Rena came down from Kiel, and we went to services at Pfarrer Bruno's church to hear his Sabbath sermon. Bruno was not a preacher who projected holy condescension to his flock. His was an intimate sharing, an invitation to his congregation to listen in for a while to Pastor Namgalies's own stream of consciousness, as it were, to set them an example. His subject was *Verzeihung,* forgiveness.

"*Er muss wachsen und ich muss kleiner werden,*" he preached. "God must grow greater in me and I must grow smaller. I must recognize the frailty of living up to my own principles. I must forgive myself when the best in me lapses and fails."

I did not need to understand every German word of his God Consciousness. I was moved as much by his tone. I could not help but juxtapose Rabbi Benny's sermon to forgive others for their sins against us, not for their sake alone, but most of all for our own, and Pfahrer Bruno's sermon that we must first forgive ourselves for our sins against others. I looked about me and saw the rapt faces of Bruno's flock beaming with inspiration and respect. The whole of my family that my mother left behind in Germany had disappeared in Hitler's boxcars. Now, Ursula and Bruno offered themselves as a surrogate family of my very own, because I was the daughter of Lotte, much loved friend of their youth.

CHAPTER 5

A Tale of Til

Bruno brought home a friend during my convalescence, a tall, gaunt man he introduced with great deference as Herr Fey, explaining that he was a puppeteer planning to produce a show based on an American theme and thought I might help him with some questions of authenticity.

"We don't too often have Americans in Mölln," Herr Fey said. "Bruno thought I might get some suggestions."

We talked a while. I didn't feel that I helped him much, but he thanked me, wished me a speedy recovery, and left.

"He is far too modest to say only that he is a puppeteer," Bruno said. "Fritz Fey is a great artist, the most famous puppet maker in Germany."

Days later, Bruno told me that Herr Fey found my ideas helpful, and he wished to thank me by inviting me, when I was strong enough, to come to his studio.

"It is a great honor," Bruno said.

Bruno took me for my first walk around the lovely medieval village of Mölln, unscathed by war. Of course, I asked him for his recollections of my grandfather.

"When I asked Ursula to marry me, she did not commit herself until she presented me for inspection to the professor."

"Not to her parents?"

"Yes, but your grandfather's approval came first. It mattered more to her. The Wachsners were having a big party the night she took me to meet him. You saw in his face a most cultured man, and very strict. I knew I was going to have to pass muster and earn his respect if I was to get his blessing. It will interest you to know that Herbert came too, that night, at your mother's invitation."

I waited for Bruno to tell me more, but passersby in the street, friends and acquaintances, members of Bruno's congregation, greeted us. They made eye contact and had a friendly smile for me, too, although I had the impression that Germans tend to hold strangers at arm's length until they feel comfortable enough to trust them. I think everyone in the village knew I was the American daughter of an old Berlin friend of Bruno and Ursula's from before the war.

"The doctor said you saved my life, Bruno."

He pretended my remark went right by him.

"I feel like the man who came to dinner."

He didn't know the expression.

"It means a person who comes to visit, then overextends her welcome. You've both been unbelievably kind to me. I've been very happy here. As happy as I can remember."

This earned me a big grin from him.

"Seeing you is like having Lotte here again. You will always be welcome in our house."

"So, my smile runs in the family?"

"Strikingly," he said. "Your grandfather, the professor. You have exactly the same smile. Also, Lotte's little brother," he added. "But most of all, Ma-ri-an-na, we only have to look at you to see your mother's smile. For us a bit of yesterday."

In the town square, we came to a wonderful old statue of a mischievous little medieval troublemaker who stares at you and gives the impression that he just pulled one over on you.

"You have heard of Til Eulenspiegel?" Bruno asked.

Bruno in 1972, during the making of A Tale of Til.

"Ever since I was a child. Mutti used to read me the *Tales of Til*. And Richard Strauss's '*Til Eulenspiegel and His Merry Pranks*' is one of our favorites."

There sat Til on his pedestal, court jester to the king, impatient for his next *lustige Streiche*, merry prank, against the rich and powerful. The little imp's arm was crooked on his hip, his legs crossed, and his elfin foot pointing at me.

"Til was buried here in Mölln. It is an old legend that if you rub his foot, good luck will come to you."

I rubbed Til's foot and we walked on. Soon we came to a little puppet museum dedicated exclusively to the genius of Fritz Fey. I won't say that Bruno had it consciously in mind to lead me there, for one can hardly walk around Mölln without coming upon this museum. But I see clearly in retrospect what could not have been perceived at the time, that there, at Herr Fey's puppet museum, the good luck legend of Til Eulenspiegel began to come true for me.

Glass cabinets lined the walls, displaying the most beautifully carved puppets in magnificently costumed stage settings of Wagnerian and Mozart operas, Shakespearean plays, and more. I mentioned offhandedly to Bruno that I thought Herr Fey's puppets would make stunning characters in a children's movie that adults would find equally entertaining. If only we had a story to tell, what might that be? Somewhere in the conversation that followed, we hardly realized that we had seamlessly set our cap on a theme for making a puppet movie. The subject? Til Eulenspiegel and his Merry Pranks.

Bruno drove us to our scheduled visit to Herr Fey's studio in the nearby countryside. The walls and the rafters of his workshop were strung with a display of hundreds of incredible puppets. Our idea to film *A Tale of Til* as a puppet show might have been stillborn if not for Bruno, who presented it to Herr Fey. I don't think I saw a wider smile in my life than I did that day on Herr Fey's face. A show of his puppets had never before been filmed. We began to make plans. There followed a flurry of activity, and it was Bruno himself, the pastor of Mölln, who took on the duties of production manager, clearing the way for filming and fighting our battles with the local authorities and their typical myriad German rules and regulations. With Herr Fey's workshop as our studio and the beautiful countryside of Schleswig Holstein for locations, we produced *A Tale of Til*.

The old legend of Til is a riddle. It encourages children to find their own answers to it. To do this, they must think independently. I always thought that Til, who follows no rules and who has been for almost a thousand years a legend beloved by the Germans, suggests a subdominant taste for freedom in a culture that historically had stressed conformance to authority. This funny, outrageous little scoundrel of a peasant cheated the burghers and the nobility out of their money while pretending to be a fool. In Germany today, inundated by rules and regulations for every little thing, this perennial hero, this icon of independence, Til Eulenspiegel, does not conform but defies authority, yet prevails.

Ursula and Bruno had saved my life. Now Pastor Bruno held out a fatherly hand and helped me wander into a career in film. Is there a design to events, invisible as they play out but plainly seen when looking back from the distance of time? Or is it that retrospection provides the mind with time to sort through random events and link and organize and interpret them into some rational pattern that we need if we are to make sense of the world? Before visiting Germany, I had never had a sick day in my life, but fate intervened to delay me in Mölln long enough to put down roots of my own and to show me again what it is to be surrounded and protected by family love and to belong. I took these riches with me when I said good-bye to the Namgalieses and headed straight for Berlin.

CHAPTER 6

Erica in Berlin

MY HEART WAS ON MY SLEEVE. I wanted to enter the space and the texture of the city Mutti grew up in. Even though it had been smashed and divided and rebuilt, Berlin still remained what it always was, a work in progress. Soon I would meet Erica Poch of the Four Girls from Berlin, a heroine of my girlhood. I wanted to be wide open to every impression, to talk with people, to observe and intuit and feel my way further into the German experience.

I took a little stroll and came upon a group of tourists gathered in front of an old dilapidated building. A tour guide was telling of the day the Nazis came here and closed down this place. If you didn't understand a word he was saying, you would know, just to look at it, the terror that still spills out of every door and window of this sad building, once the Jewish Girls School of Berlin. The Gestapo trucked the children to Alte Hamburgerstrasse, the deportation collection place for Jews. It was the Nazi policy to move out detainees within the hour, and the girls were sent away in boxcars rolling east long before the frantic parents ever knew their girls were missing when they failed to come home from school. One of the tourists yawned. I am sure he didn't mean to be disrespectful of what he had just heard.

It is only the simultaneity of my heartache and his yawn that gave me pause to reflect.

I wanted to go to Weissensee Cemetery to see the grave of my grandmother but discovered it was in the Soviet Zone, so, like a Berliner, I paid my fare on the honor system to a machine at the back of a trolley and rode the E-Bahn wherever it would take me, fantasizing that if I squinted my eyes, I would transmute the trolley and the city sights passing by to a time long gone when Mutti and Ursula and Erica and Ilonka rode these very trolley lines. I would see Berlin just as they saw it.

Perhaps, in my imagination, I did conjure up the old Berlin. Blood-red banners with black swastikas unfurled everywhere. But it was the Berlin of today that my eyes opened wide to, and far off down Strasse des 17. Juni, I saw the Brandenburg Gate, just as they saw it. The swastikas were gone, but strife and division remained, for just beyond it I saw what they did not, the Wall dividing East and West.

Nor in their day did the Four Girls see the same faces as today, the exotic ones on the crowded trolley in this new and vital city of ever-bustling West Berlin. Now, people of other ethnicities and races also lived here—most of all, Turks in great numbers, who were encouraged to come and earn higher wages and help to rebuild the new Germany.

Sitting next to me on the crowded trolley was a grand old matriarch in black from head to toe, her lips pursed in disapproval. She had on an old-fashioned feathered hat of the 1930s, her shoulders were thrown back, her skin a startling white, hands resting one on the other on her cane. She turned to me to catch my eye. And when she saw she had my attention, she looked about us at the Turkish faces, shook her head, and whispered audibly so that the others would hear: "Too bad we can't have our good old German Jews back again."

I was stunned. One could ponder the remark for a lifetime. Prejudice revisited. Now it was the Turks' turn. Was she speaking in fond remembrance of her "good old German Jews"? That was the most generous interpretation. Or did she mean she felt more at home with Jews to look down upon rather than these dark, foreign-speaking "others," these Turks lurking about now who, unlike the Jews, will not stand for any amount of systematic persecution. After all, the Jews were Germans who looked and felt and acted just like her. Yet they were Jewish and therefore different, and thus she could love them or hate them, depending on the periodic whims of the scapegoating leaders whose sleight of hand moved public opinion and inflamed the populace against the Jews for their own secret agendas. Hadn't Germany always relied on her Jews to accept victimhood nicely, remain true to Deutschland just the same, try all the harder to show their loyalty, and come back ready for more? A heartless syndrome, as anyone familiar with German Jewish history would readily agree.

I wish I had told the old lady in the plumed hat what I thought of her remark. I wish I had asked her why she wasn't outraged in the first place when her "good old German Jewish" neighbors were forced from their homes and herded into the streets, never to be seen again. And why wasn't it enough to want them back today just because they came from here and belonged, no less than she? Why wasn't the persecution of any German an affront to her and to all Germans? Why wasn't the German love of justice powerful enough for her to regret their ghosts? Why not do right in the first place rather than need to "make good again"? I wish I had asked her these things. I ask myself why I didn't and why hadn't I vented my constructive indignation on the old woman in the hospital and tried to press her gently, if insistently, into a dialogue? A person ought to do that out of self-respect. One ought to take every opportunity that comes along to practice *tikkun olam*; the Hebrew words mean "to improve the world." If you don't express your ideas when you can't be thrown in prison or killed for them, how can you point your finger at people who didn't when the consequences were heinous? All this swirled round and round in my mind while I rode on a tram in the heart of Berlin, taking a pilgrimage to the past.

My family had passed through the Brandenburg Gate, generation after generation. Just beyond it is Stalin's Wall and the wide boulevard once called Unter Den Linden. Mutti talked a lot about Berlin as her health waned and death was close at hand, replaying random images of a treasured youth.

103

"Nearby to Unter Den Linden and Friedrichstrasse, in that part of Berlin called die Mitte, the City Center, is Hackescher Markt, where, on Rosenthalerstrasse, the finest shirts in Europe were made in my uncle Heinrich's factory."

She talked about the day the Nazis came to power. I always wanted to know what it actually felt like to be in Berlin when the darkest evil in history was given the power to govern. Many decades had passed, but not long enough ago to reduce the fear it brought to her face. Such a sad smile. When I think of that smile, a word I can't remember ever having learned or used rises to consciousness: *weltschmerz*. A direct translation means "world pain." In the vernacular, it means "woebegone" or "disconsolate," and such was the tone of her reply. Her English soon trailed off into a German stream of consciousness. History as it happened.

"An ordinary Monday morning. I met Erica in the street. She lived nearby and we usually walked to school together. Test scores were to be posted for an exam I took the Friday before. I was eager to see my grades. At Wilhelmstrasse, an odd feeling came over me, a latent sense of foreboding, a certain disquietude. Something in the air.

"In school, it was not yet noon when the class was interrupted by whispering around the room. Then, suddenly, Hitler's name was on everyone's lips. He had been appointed chancellor. My heart sank. The professor tried to continue his lecture, but he could not keep order. The class broke up and we went outside. The whole school filled the halls and overflowed into the street where Erica and Ursula and I found one another. Students were milling about. Many of our classmates were celebrating. I could not believe they felt this way. Ursula did not care much about politics, but she was all excited just the same, and Erica kept repeating, 'It can't be true.' They were embarrassed in front of me. I was embarrassed, too."

"Why were you embarrassed, Mom?" I asked.

"We never talked about our religions, other than I went to church once with Ursula for Christmas, and she came to temple with me, too. She liked Hanukkah and Passover. All my friends were welcome at our Passover seders. I was proud of my faith, but it was a private thing. Now, being Jewish had me under a spotlight. I was ashamed that they felt offended for me, sorry for me. It was awkward for all of us.

"We went to my house. Paula was already listening to the news. It was on every station. The announcer was excited and shrieking that President Von Hindenburg had appointed Hitler chancellor. The day before, Von Schleicher had resigned his post as chancellor and it had been expected that the president would give his support to Von Papen to replace him, not Hitler. Erica went off on a tirade, calling him 'that charismatic sociopathic ignorant loudmouth who now will misrepresent our Germany in front of the world. Hindenburg is a good man. Why would he give us Hitler? How could he do such a thing?'

"I was excited, too, and depressed, all rolled together in a confusing rage that wanted to explode. Erica said she was going home to be with her parents. Paula told her to be careful, that it was much wiser these days, especially when outside, to keep one's thoughts to oneself. Paula wanted me to stay home. We went out again anyway and walked Erica home. Her father also told us to go home. So Ursula and I went out and walked down Friedrichstrasse.

"The atmosphere was charged. The streets were filling with sightseers. The sidewalk was jammed at the Kaiserhoff Hotel. We could hardly get by. Newsreel trucks were parked up and down the street, and cables and lights were being set up, and we heard people say that Hitler was inside. The crowd was shoving and elbowing for the big moment when he would make his appearance. I felt eyes on me, examining me. I knew we had better keep moving.

"In the Tiergarten, Nazis were already gathering for a big parade. It felt awful to see the great number of cheering well-wishers siding with evil. Here and there, a few familiar faces showing their true colors, Berliners who heard Hitler's anti-Semitic ranting and could live with it. The patriotic zeal was contagious, overpowering. Ursula was drawn into it. I, too, was attracted and repelled by it. But for me it was all the more depressing because I was a patriot, too, and not welcome to participate with them in this fantastic, repugnant day in our country's history. I wanted to crawl into the safety of a cocoon and suffer my angst in private.

"Ursula tried to walk me back home. I said it wasn't necessary. I felt like a stranger in my own neighborhood. I hastened down the street. My father was always in his lecture hall at this hour, but he had come home, too. Ilonka telephoned and said not to worry, that Hitler was all bluster and sooner or later we would see the last of him. And Benny showed up, paying calls on his congregants to discuss the situation, urging everyone to stay calm and keep what had happened in proper perspective. He sat down beside Papa and Paula and me, listening, mesmerized, to the radio.

"The widespread celebration of Hitler's triumph surprised us like a slap in the face. We were worried about Mops. Where was he? We expected him to come right home. I had never before been afraid for the physical safety of my family. We breathed easier when he came home. He said nothing and went to his room and shut the door. I don't think I ever saw him depressed before, but his country had been handed to a devil whose intentions were malevolent, if you believed what he said, which not many of us Jews did until later.

"We knew of Jew-hating acts around the city. We hardly expected them to get worse. Soon you didn't have to pay your bills anymore if you owed Jewish doctors and other professionals. Jewish judges were thrown off the bench, followed by the boycotting of Jewish stores. The boycott didn't work. It was much more important to people that they continue to patronize their favorite stores than to hate the shop owners whom they had long trusted and had been doing business with for years. The next day the Nazis called it off. It goes to show you what could have been if everybody had said no to Hitler's anti-Semitism. So, it went downhill from there. Jews were thrown out of the civil service. We could not go anymore to public swimming pools, and they threw us off sports teams."

Effective immediately at school, every class began with "Heil Hitler." Mutti found her arm lifting in salute just the same as her fellow students, some of whom ardently thrust out their arms. She loathed them for it, and even though she had no choice but to comply, she hated herself as much. Soon, quotas were introduced for Jewish students in schools. The next day, Mutti and Erica were out walking

106

when students from the university marched down Unter Den Linden singing anti-Semitic songs.

"So much for the youth of the world defending civilization," Erica yelled at them. Mutti was shaking. She begged Erica to be quiet.

"One privilege after another was withdrawn," Mutti said, "and it kept on getting worse. In August, Jews could no longer swim at Wansee Lake, Jewish actors and musicians were forbidden to work in their professions, and more. And this was just the beginning. Who could think the unthinkable, perhaps not even Hitler himself, that soon he would decide to actually go ahead and kill all the Jews of Europe?

"Der Alte Fritz roiled with anger. Try to imagine being cut from the flock, being told you no longer are entitled to love your country, that your patriotism no longer belongs to you, that your Germanness was a fraud, and you had been stripped of it?

"Mops came home one day. A troop of Hitler Youth had accosted him and spat on him and called him a 'dirty Jew.' One of them from school said Mops was his 'good dirty Jew,' so they let him go. They might just as soon have beaten him in the street. It made you think twice before going outside. But you had to go out. We adapted to danger. It became an everyday part of life. But Mops wasn't taking the encounter in his stride. He said it didn't feel like his country anymore. To say this was a real assault on Papa's patriotic sensibilities.

"'This is our Deutschland,' Papa enunciated. 'Even more so when our Deutschland needs citizens who still think. They know very well what they stand to lose without us. We will remain calm in our *Heimat*, homeland. We will keep a low profile and wait and see.' Keeping a low profile had been, since time immemorial, the mantra of the Jews of Germany. It was my father's final word on the matter. We kept the radio on the rest of the day and far into the night. The sky glowed over Berlin with the torchlights of the parades. It was terrible, schizophrenic, to live in two worlds, fascinated by the pageantry, yet repelled by the Neanderthal fervor of our fellow *Landsleute*.

"'But things got worse. Mops came home with a medallion, and he took it out of his pocket and held it up for us to see. On one side was a Star of David, on the other, a swastika. Papa knew how he came

Mops at age fifteen, 1935.

by it. Newsstands all over the city were distributing them in connection with favorable articles in the Nazi press about young German Jewish pioneers who had left for Palestine. The Nazi travel reporter had journeyed to the Holy Land to interview them. The articles were very complimentary, commending the Jews for working the land, openly admiring them for building the Jewish state and fulfilling the dream of Theodore Herzl.

"'You're always talking about what our country needs,' Mops said. 'Whose country? Theirs, Papa? What Germany needs is for us Jews to get out. I know some boys whose families are leaving for Palestine. What are we waiting for?' He was treading on dangerous ground. My father was not a Zionist. Nor was Benny. They were both German Nationalists. It must have taken all Mops had to face up to such authority.

"'We should go, too,' he insisted.

"Your grandfather's response was controlled and confident. 'We should not. You think we can abandon who we are and what we are. I did not hide from danger in 1915 when my country went to war.

Our duty to our country is no less now. It does not need us to cower before bullies. No one can budge us out of our birthright.'"

"What did you think, Mom?" I asked.

"I thought the same as my father and Benny. Mops lost his sense of humor that day. He saw clearer what the family should do. If only my father had listened. Mops changed from a boy to a man under the pressure of events. He was proud of who he was and felt no more apologetic for being a Jew than a German Catholic or Lutheran feels self-conscious about their religions. He wasn't interested at all in 'keeping a low profile.' Papa was the patriarch of the extended family. If you had a problem, you brought it to Fritz. He would fix it. Such a man would not leave Germany without them. I had three grand-mothers. How could he move his mother, a woman of eighty-eight, out of the land she loved, or Paula's mother, or my mother's mother, and aunts and uncles and cousins, a whole clan? My father would have left, kicking and screaming, only if the last of them preceded him."

All this ran like a loop in my mind as the bus crossed into the Britischer Sektor and down Kurfurstendamm. I got off a few blocks from Erica's address in fashionable Charlottenburg and found my way to her street. She hadn't known just when to expect me, and she wasn't at home, so I sat on her steps to wait and must have dozed because, in a while, someone was shaking my shoulder. I opened my eyes to a woman with thick-rimmed glasses scrutinizing me with a critical eye from head to toe.

"You are your mother's daughter," she said in flawless English, without the faintest indecision about who I was. It was as if she had known me all my life, which, of course, from Mutti's letters, she had. "You look just like her. One can hardly hope you sing like her as well."

"Nothing to match my mother's," I replied. I had time-traveled to meet a living legend. Here, in the flesh, was another of the Four Girls from Berlin, Erica Poch herself. She was just as I imagined her to be, no great beauty, but she had a puckish, mischievous, fun-loving, direct way about her that Mutti had always described and I was about to discover. Her energy was fantastic. She was classically educated yet street-smart, and, most of all, still an independent woman who thought

109

Lotte with her three grandmothers, Apolant, Pese, and Wachsner, 1937.

for herself and wasn't afraid to let you know. Such a woman as that had managed to survive Nazism and Communism, so this was saying a mouthful.

"I will show you Berlin, but you are too pale. With *Gelbsucht*, six months is not enough time to get back on your feet. Ursula told me ten times to make sure that you rest every day. I will see to it that you get enough rest, and I will fatten you up."

That night was the exception. We sat in her beautiful apartment and talked and talked until the wee hours, and first, she wanted to know all about Mutti.

"She's fine," I answered.

Erica cut through the chit-chat in a hurry. "I am fine. She is fine. You are fine. In America, everybody is fine. So I will ask of you again, how is your mother?"

"Okay, she smokes too much. She says she is quitting but never does. Cigarettes and coffee for breakfast, and for supper, cigarettes and coffee and a piece of pie."

"So, she still loves her coffee, but to smoke is not good for the body, not good for the voice. Lotte's voice. A voice that took you by surprise every time you heard it. It captured your attention, your emotions. I was at Ilonka's, waiting for my lesson when I first heard her voice. It wasn't a voice. It was a phenomenon. It seemed to float through the walls of the studio and hang on its own echo. I could not tell what direction it came from, something like a ventriloquist throwing his voice. Why didn't she pursue her career in America?"

"I don't think she had the will without her father to cheer her on."

"She was an artist. Why did she become a nurse?"

"She almost died in Westerbork Detention Camp in Holland. That's where she wound up when the *St. Louis* returned to Europe. I won't mention the indignities she endured in the camp. It surely didn't do her voice any good. But that's where she got interested in nursing. She thought that if she was going to die there, at least she might try to do some good."

"Yes, that is Lotte for you," Erica said.

"Everyone knew it was a matter of time before Hitler would invade Holland. It was as if she was trapped behind barbed wire to be held in custody for Hitler until he could lay his hands on her. The only way Lotte knew how to give meaning to her situation was to throw herself into something positive. So she began looking after the children and nursing the sick and elderly. It gave her the sense of purpose she needed to go on. Otherwise, I don't think she would have made it. She found that she was good at nursing. It redeemed her. She got her credentials after she came to America. If she hadn't had nursing and me in her life, she wouldn't have had the will to live. In all these years, haven't you women ever talked to each other about these things?"

"*Hör mal gut zu*, Ma-ri-an-na. Listen carefully, young lady, we 'women' read each other very well, including between the lines. So don't get me started."

"I'm here to get you started."

"All right, then, if that is what you want. A lot of Germans said they never knew what Hitler was doing. Or they admit they got themselves into bed with Hitler."

I said, "But when they saw what was happening, they didn't know how to get themselves out."

*Lotte in Griffith Park,
Los Angeles, 1950.*

Lotte (far right) with her coworkers at Kaiser Permanente in Hollywood, 1952.

"Don't be an apologist."

"I'm not an apologist. Not in the least. But if I am ever to understand what happened, I want to see clearly, and what I see is blame enough to go all the way around."

Erica flushed on the sudden recall of a moment that cut Lotte to the quick and reflected the gradual transformation in social life that Nazism imposed on Germany.

"Lotte was so popular. There were other girls besides us who were her friends whose friendships disappeared after 1933. She was deeply wounded to find how false they were."

The same pressures put to the test the vulnerabilities and attitudes of many of my grandfather's friends. Feelings were bound to shift when old colleagues were forced by mortal danger to confront their own latent prejudices, which the state encouraged. But, for the time being, my grandfather was still held in high esteem in the world of academia.

"It must have been 1934," Erica said. "A discussion group of young philosophy students were arguing around the dining room table about what they thought the philosopher Ludwig Wittgenstein was saying. Dr. Wachsner, as always, served as moderator. The doorbell rang. Lotte and I looked out the window and saw a late arrival at the door, a student whom we'd known as a friend for years. Maximilian Thiel was his name. We watched as he took a swastika pin off his lapel before Klarchen opened the door to let him in. Lotte's jaw dropped, literally. I could have killed him. I felt betrayed. Max, who was one of Professor Wachsner's own students and the best, came into the dining room, apologizing to no end for his tardiness. It was a contradiction neither of us could get out of our minds, giving himself and his talent and energy over to a system that hated the Jews while sustaining the profoundest respect for the professor, all bound in one. In those days there often were such opposing ideologies oddly coexisting in the same person. Didn't they see how conflicted that was? Nothing has changed. I find myself wondering about it still."

I told Erica about the old woman on the tram, and my hospital roommate. "I'll always wonder about it, too," Erica said. "I will never understand it. When the war was over, to hear us Germans tell it, there was not a Nazi in Germany. Nobody even knew a Nazi. Everybody had a story to tell you about the Jew they kept hidden in their basement. But I don't forget the ardor of us Germans—doctors, lawyers, businessmen, the indifference of the churches. So much for education and human reason and the teachings of religion. All have Jewish blood on their hands."

"It doesn't go away, does it?"

"How can it go away when not a word about it is taught in school, no curriculum at all. Enough now about those days. You just got here."

"It's what I came for."

"We will lift ourselves up and change the subject."

Just as Lotte said, Erica was still that strong personality, outspoken in her opinions and expressing them passionately. She had a surprise in mind. It was typical of her to come up with the unexpected.

"And what does every woman want to do when she comes to a new city?"

"I don't know. What does a woman want to do when she comes to a new city?"

"She wants to shop, of course. We are going to Ka De We, and we will look in the shops on the Kurfurstendamm and have lunch at . . . never mind, I will keep that my secret."

Here is my journal entry. It is as vivid as yesterday: "Kurfurstendamm. Elegant. Cross between 5th Ave. and Wilshire Blvd. Bombed out KaiserWilhelmKirche, memorial to the result of war. Right by is Ka De We. Love this store. Class act. Est. old Berlin. Mentioned to Erica that Lotte and Ursula were here when a parade of Hitler Youth came down the Kurfurstendamm.

"What? They didn't tell you I was here, too?" Erica laughed. "That boy with the flag who tripped. It surely wasn't me he was falling over."

"Crazy about a purse. Gorgeous. Very major bucks. She insists on getting it for me. Certainly not. Implores me. Wants me to have 'something special to make up for all your birthdays.' Says would have been at every one of them. I can't accept. Hurts her feelings. I feel bad."

Erica was now the head of a leading school of music in West Berlin. She hadn't always had it this good. When the war ended, she was living in East Berlin, the sector of the city occupied by the Soviets. The Cold War began, and she was trapped there for years after the Russians built the Wall. She took tyranny of any stripe as a personal insult.

"They turned my stomach with the swastika. Now it was the hammer and sickle. I would have faced very serious consequences if they'd caught me trying to get over the Wall."

To Erica, "getting over" to the other side meant being patient and working the system. She rose in rank and became the headmistress of a music school for the children of political luminaries. When the time came, she didn't have to try to go over the Wall. She made it through with the proper papers. I asked her how she managed to do it.

"Never mind that," she said. "The less said, the better."

In West Berlin, Erica again persevered and became the principal of a music academy. She was very successful. I only needed to be patient and listen and I'd hear much from her about the old days. She said a great singing voice needed to be combined with great ambition to make a career, and it was true that my grandfather had pushed Lotte from the onset. Erica also said that my mother needed to be pushed. Nudged gently but firmly was the better way to put it. Mutti had no aggressiveness of her own. She was so gentle, she brought out the protector in the girls.

"I'm sure she makes a most excellent nurse. She was the best at everything she ever did. But nursing is not for her. Not with a talent like that. No matter what, she should have stayed with singing. She had a rare instrument. She was an artist. Plenty of music in that house. Always bringing musicians home for dinner, especially if they were students. That is how your mother met your father. Interesting people, artists, businessmen, intellectuals, everybody was crazy about the professor. Lively debates on every subject you can imagine. Of course, politics. I loved to hear Professor Wachsner discourse.

"Somebody was saying that perhaps it was true after all, that we Germans need a strong leader like that Hitler fellow coming up in the popularity polls, someone who will pull our country up as the great power in Europe it deserves to be. Your grandfather told him when Herr Hitler speaks of 'our' country, he does not mean the Jews. He said that if only we had 'checks and balances' in government, nothing could go wrong. The man hadn't known what that meant. Nor had I. The professor explained that it was the American concept of government that protected the rule of law by spreading power between the judiciary, the legislative, and the executive branches of government in a balanced way that none of them could usurp. The man said he thought we had all that in the Weimar constitution. 'A constitution is no stronger than a government that will uphold it. If Adolf Hitler comes to power, you can kiss it good-bye.' Prophetic words. They had a lasting impression on me. Having freedom and keeping it are two different things. Hitler taught us that. One learns much better what liberty is when it is taken from you. We soon enough learned what it is to live without it."

Erica spoke in a monotone as she remembered Dr. Wachsner, the professor of chemistry and biology, discoursing one night on a pet theory of his.

" 'We carry a savage gene,' he said, 'the result of natural selection in the primordial soup in which life began, that pitted microorganisms, one against the other. Millions of years later, we crawled onto land and became tribe against tribe for the available supply of food and living space. Modern man has polished himself now, but a nicer patina does not mean we have changed much inside. We still kill for markets and lebensraum (living space). Our savage gene is the Achilles' heel of the human race because we hunt our prey among our own species. Because of this, no human being can depend upon help arriving from his fellow human beings in his hour of need.' Your grandfather believed that to own up to this was a positive step to take, no matter how begrudgingly. It gave us our one and only chance, maybe, to someday break through. This inevitably turned the discussion to Darwinism versus the Bible, but he said he thought evolution was a perfectly elegant way for God to have created the universe. I don't think he ever had the chance to apply the scientific method to his theory, but I believed in it then as I believe in it now, with all my heart."

"Do you remember a Rabbi Benno Gottschalk?"

"Remember him? Of course, I do. Lotte always sends me his best. We would sit around for hours and listen to the deep discussions he had with your grandfather. Some things you cannot forget. He said the Lord did not finish His work when He made the world. He gave humans free choice to help Him improve the world as a work in progress. Or choose not to. Without the power to choose between good and evil, we could be neither."

"That's his favorite sermon. It's called *Tikkun Olam*, to heal the world. 'God did not make us robots, because a machine cannot choose between good and evil. God made us with free will so that we would know the difference. Good comes not from overcoming evil, but from doing battle with all your heart.' Benny would look me in the eyes and ask me, 'Do you know the difference?' His question comes to mind when I'm about to act. Sometimes I forget. I suppose it means not the destination but the trip."

To celebrate my "return to Berlin," which was, in Erica's mind, my natural habitat, the "special surprise" she had in mind was lunch at the famous old Berlin restaurant Kempinski's. She got us a nice table.

"Kempinski's was the favorite place of the Nazi bigwigs because the food was great, which, as you'll see, it still is, and also because when Mr. Kempinski presented his bill to the Party, they laughed in his face and refused to pay because Mr. Kempinski was Jewish. And still they kept on coming just the same, day in and day out, for years to stuff their fat bellies."

Erica waited for dessert and, with it, served me up a delight that wasn't on the menu, an incident I had only just heard about from Ursula, but with a different twist.

"Would it interest you to know that forty years ago Ilonka took your mother and Ursula and me to Kempinski's for lunch? I think it was 1932 or '33."

"We overheard three Nazis who were gorging themselves at the next table. 'Too many Jews,' one of them said. They were loudmouths who meant to be heard. One of them was slurping his chicken soup, a very fat, bald man. Nearby diners heard the remark but ignored it and went on eating. But everything stopped at our table. Your mother was nervous because Ursula was very unpredictable and there was no telling what she might do. Ilonka felt responsible for us and tried to calm things down by ignoring them and went right on with our conversation. But hardly had she continued when one of the Nazis yelled, 'Too many Jews at the top.' Ursula stood up. The bigots' eyes swiveled to us. Ominous grins broke out on their faces. 'Too many Jews from the top to the bottom,' one of them said. 'But not for long,' the fat man added and drew his finger across his throat.

"Now, Ilonka was a lady who believed in proper public demeanor and expected the same from us. But Ursula had risen from her seat, so Ilonka pushed her back down and shouted, 'Why don't you use a real knife?' surprised by her own bravura, and added out loud that we should pay no attention to these riffraff and not give ourselves nervous stomachs when we were eating. 'Don't worry, I am under control,' Ursula said calmly, and daintily patted her mouth with her napkin, stood up, and stepped over to their table. Now, Ursula was a Nordic beauty and towered over the Nazis like Brunhilde in all her Teutonic splendor.

"'Why do you want to eat Herr Kempinski's food if you feel that way?' she asked.

"'Food's great,' grinned the fat man as he guzzled his soup.

"'Then why not have a little takeout, *du Fettsack*, you lardbag,' she said and tipped his bowl of hot soup into his lap. He jumped to his feet, sopping wet and raging. Ursula laughed in his face. The strange thing was, his fellow Nazis were laughing, too. Lotte's heart was beating in her chest. You could see the thumping on her blouse. We were relieved when they just got up and left."

"Ursula said that you did it. You're the one who spilled the soup."

Erica talked right on through me.

"A year or two later, it would have ended a lot more seriously for us all," she said.

We drove to Wansee and Potsdam and took the bus to Caputh, just as the girls had done all those years ago when Mutti met Herbert. I happened to ask Erica whether the building Mutti lived in had been destroyed. A sudden fury flashed in her eyes.

"Come, I will show you."

Erica drove west through Berlin on the Kurfurstendamm, turned left at the Kempinski Hotel, and passed by the landmark Fassenenstrasse Synagogue, known throughout Germany, on the steps of which Kaiser Wilhelm himself appeared on the day of its consecration.

"The synagogue was completely gutted on Kristallnacht, the night of broken glass," Erica said. "The Nazis flooded the sanctuary with gasoline. Crowds gathered on the street to watch as the flames consumed it. It was a magnificent building. The fire department came, but they watched, too. Their orders were to step in and confine the flames only if the fire threatened the adjacent buildings. That night, they set fire to synagogues all over Germany. You could not drive in Berlin the next day. Wherever you went, the streets were littered with layer upon layer of broken glass from the windows of Jewish shops."

"Where was Lotte that day?"

"She stayed home."

Today, a column is all that remains of the Fassanenstrasse Synagogue. The new Jewish Community Center and library stands there now. On future trips I would find my grandfather's telephone number there, listed in the Berlin telephone book until the 1939 edition, from which it disappeared.

Soon we came to Mutti's old neighborhood.

"There were buildings here and there that weren't leveled, sometimes a whole block," Erica said as she turned onto Schapperstrasse and pulled up to the curb. "Here we are. This is where we spent so much of our time. Schapperstrasse, Number 30."

She pointed to a window. "Lotte was married here, you know. Your father left for Cuba the same day. That was in December of 1938. Lotte left six months later, in May of 1939. From then on, I came on Tuesdays, once a week, and Ilonka on Thursdays, to check on the Wachsners. This continued for nearly three years. There was nothing we could do but see to it that they had enough to eat. Look, there across the street, a shoe repair sign still hangs. Everything is almost as it was. If you didn't know it, you might think you were back in old Berlin."

Erica said to take my time. I got out of the car and stood on the sidewalk and looked up at Schapperstrasse 30. I squinted my eyes and tried to imagine Mutti and Der Alte Fritz and Paula and my Uncle Mops and Benny and Ursula and Erica and Ilonka walking in and out of this very doorway not all that long ago.

For no reason at all, I walked across Schapperstrasse and down a flight of stairs to the little basement shoe repair shop. I asked the old shoemaker if he happened to remember a family named Wachsner who had once lived across the street. He wanted to know what my interest was. I said my mother knew them once, a long time ago.

"I had a customer by that name," he said, "a professor who came to me for years with their shoes."

As if someone might overhear, he lowered his voice. "They were Jews, you know, so I did a little something extra to make their soles last as long as possible."

My heart was beating so fast. I hadn't expected to find anybody who remembered my family. I asked him what else he remembered. He shook his head.

"Too bad about the son," he said. He came in a few times. I had to be careful."

I froze in mid-stride. What did he say? My blood pounded in my head. My legs urged me to run. I asked the old shoemaker what he meant.

"He was hiding someplace nearby." The shoemaker looked toward the door and again he dropped his voice, as if he still could face punishment. "The Russians came right through Schapperstrasse and down those steps, pointing their machine guns at me. They would have shot me on the spot, no doubt, had I not been a cobbler. They got everyone out of the buildings. He was there among them, milling about on the street. They shot the men and took away the women. They would have shot me, too, if they didn't need me to mend their boots."

Erica, 1945.

It was pure happenstance for Erica to have mentioned the shoe-maker. Had she not, I would not have thought to inquire there. Or the old shoemaker might not have remembered this incident. Looking back, the irony of it all, once again, seemed like a designed progression of events that had no purpose other than for me to stumble upon the answer to Mops's fate. He had come out of hiding to greet the conquering saviors just in time to regain full equality with his fellow countrymen before the Russians shot him down in the street with the rest of them. I admit I still harbor the fantasy of waking up one day and finding him alive, for in Mops, Mutti had bestowed upon me the contour of an ephemeral uncle whom I made flesh, only for reality to now snatch him back into ghostly form. I got back into the car and told Erica.

"Ernst," she sighed. "Well, now we know. Lotte loved him most of all."

It began as a slow boil, and soon Erica was upset all over again. She said she still didn't know what to do with her indignation.

Grandfather Fritz with an album containing his flora and fauna drawings, in the early 1940s.

Paula and Fritz, also in the early 1940s, when they feared the worst.

"After Lotte left, Ilonka and I watched over the Wachsners as best we could. My father planted a vegetable garden behind our house. Everything was rationed by then. There were many foods that Jews were no longer allowed to have. We would go to the professor's house wearing our longest coats. Underneath, we hid the necessities of life. I brought them fresh vegetables from our garden. Meat when we could. Ilonka brought her own ration of fruit. It was not so pleasant a thing to watch such people brought low. Once, I smuggled out a manuscript of his."

"'Gotteskampf.'"

"Ja, that was the title. If I had been caught with it, I don't have to tell you."

"He was a great man," I said.

"That is the right word for him. He was a great man. And Frau Wachsner. Paula. So sweet a nature, so generous and kind, a quiet person, so gentle. She ran that household, you know. Handled all of the accounts, and she made sure there always was plenty of money ready when the professor had the chance to acquire a rare stamp for his collection. It broke my heart to see such a lovely woman frightened, more and more so after Lotte left. They knew the day would come when they too would hear a knocking on their door. Toward the end, she seemed calm. She gave herself over to her fate. You can be proud to have had her for your grandmother."

I thanked her for that and for the carton, but she was not one to take bows. She shook her head. She didn't want to talk about the carton, but I just needed to let her know what an overwhelming impact it had on my life.

People from all walks of life were drawn to my grandfather. He had powerful connections and had thought no one would touch him. Even after the Nuremberg Laws, he chose to remain in Germany, stripped of his legal standing as a citizen, rather than leave. Nothing that Lotte said would make him budge, not even pointing out the excellent life he could make for himself elsewhere. He said it was dishonorable to desert his country "just when it needed its true defenders more than ever."

Erica told me he was always poring over his stamp collection with a big magnifying glass.

"He often asked me which stamp struck my fancy and I always picked the prettiest. Then he rattled off everything there was to know about that stamp, the whole history, and he could do this for every one of those thousands of stamps in his collection. Remember, stamps occupied only one small area of his interest."

"I wonder what became of his collection."

"I know what became of it. He sold some stamps to pay for your parents' transportation to Cuba. He had quietly been selling them off for some time. No one knew this, not even your mother. But I knew, because my father was the go-between. After Kristallnacht, the dealers began to take advantage of the professor's situation, so every few months, as an Aryan, my father would take a stamp and sell it for the professor at its real market value. That's what kept them going. It was like withdrawing money from a bank account, which Jews could no longer have. Toward the end, someone high in the SS, a former student of his, offered to do him a favor and take the collection off his hands for a pittance, pointing out that if he didn't make up his mind fast enough, the price would go down by the next day. But most of his collection had been sold off by then."

"What do you mean, 'Toward the end'?" I asked.

She dabbed at a tear. "The SS man got what was left, but it wasn't much. It didn't help them. The Jews were told to keep a suitcase ready. The Wachsners each had one all packed by the door. The suitcases stood there for a long time. Three years. I came one day and the suitcases were gone. You wanted to know. Now you know."

Erica got us through a checkpoint into the Soviet Zone without delay and drove to Weissensee Cemetery to visit my grandmother's grave. It was still chained off and unkempt and overgrown. We couldn't get in. Just the same, outside the gates to the huge old Jewish cemetery in Berlin seemed as appropriate a place as any to say Kaddish, the Jewish prayer for the dead, for my family at the funeral they never had.

Lotte had long since accepted that Mops disappeared in the huge graveyard that was Europe. Erica and I both agreed that there was no point in ever telling her. Erica showed me more of Berlin, but the funereal mood hung over us. I made no further entries in my journal the rest of my time with her. Not until I got home and unpacked my suitcase and found the fabulous purse from Ka De We that Erica had tucked inside.

CHAPTER 7

Lotte's Love

I EXPECTED TO GET TOGETHER WITH LOTTE the night I came home, but she was now the surgeons' first-choice nurse at Kaiser Permanente in Hollywood, and she had an emergency call. As soon as our schedules permitted, I went to her apartment on Kenmore Avenue and found her in the middle of her favorite meal. She still couldn't be bothered with real food if she was the one who had to prepare it. I toyed with the idea of not finding fault with her the first time we were together after such a long time apart. Then I decided that it was irresponsible if I did not.

"The worst thing is coffee and pie. What kind of nourishment do you think that is? At night, yet, before you go to sleep."

"Who sleeps?"

"Not to mention the smoking. Why do I have to keep carping at you about these things?"

"You don't. Please remember, I am the medical authority in this house."

She got up and came over and took my pulse. "*Um Gottes willen*, for heaven's sake, your body is still recuperating. You cannot be running all day, day in and day out, the way you do. After *Gelbsucht*, it takes time to rebuild one's strength."

My mother gave me a hug and a kiss. She was eager for a full report. I said the country of her birth was stunning. I told her that the doctor credited Ursula and Bruno with saving my life. She wanted to know about their homes. They were truly lovely, and I described them to her. There was that moment, just a flash, in which we both knew she found her surroundings wanting by comparison. I told her about Bruno and Herr Fey and the film we made of Til. I showed her Ursula's linocut of Mölln and told her that Erica had taken me to Kempinski's and to see her old building at Schapperstrasse, 30.

"On the way, Erica drove past a synagogue that was gutted during Kristallnacht."

"On Johannestrasse?" Mutti shot back.

"I don't know. It was on a street off a main drag, Kurfursten-damm."

"That would have been the Fassenenstrasse Synagogue. Rabbi Leo Baeck's temple."

"Erica said you stayed home on Kristallnacht, which is more than you ever told me."

"What is there to say? They did it in the dead of night. In the morning I smelled the smoke that hung over the city, and yes, I stayed home. My father went out. His face was white when he came back. He shut the door behind him and locked it as if to shut out the destruction he saw on the street. The window displays at Ka De We were smashed and looted. Wertheim's, too, and all the big department stores. Every street was littered with broken glass. You couldn't drive a car in fear of slashing your tires. Papa stood there, staring at the door. He unlocked it and threw it open again, closed it, opened it, closed it, and locked it again. I asked him what he was doing.

"'A door used to keep the outside from entering a person's sacred domain. Now, a door is just a piece of wood on hinges. Utterly useless against any ruffian who wants to come in.' He plopped down in his favorite chair. A pack of cigarettes appeared out of his pocket and with an elegant flourish, he took one out, lit it, and began puffing on it. The thing of it is, he'd never smoked before."

I told Lotte we had gone to Weissensee Cemetery to visit her mother's grave, but it was still chained off and we couldn't get in. She said it was hard to think I had been right there where Der Alte Fritz used to take her as a little girl once a week to tend the flower garden they had planted on her mother's grave. How odd it was that she has rested there since 1915, but there were no graves for the people who buried her.

"Ursula told me quite a lot about Herbert and you."

"I am sure you are the one who brought it up."

"How you met him on the train to Caputh with your singing group."

"A lovely time. Another life," she said with finality, closing the door to the subject for the time being. I never told her Ursula thought that had she and Herbert married, he just might have been able to do something about getting them all out.

Mutti phoned me on my birthday. She said she thought she needed a hamburger and fries for dinner before taking on a large slab of the birthday cake she had waiting for me, all to be washed down with a couple of cups of black coffee, followed by a Chesterfield. So that night, on the way to her apartment, I got some takeout at Hamburger Hamlet and put it on the table with a nice merlot. We lit candles, feasted on junk food, sipped wine, and were chatting away when all at once I realized she had seamlessly segued back into the story of the great love of her life.

"My father didn't speak Yiddish, but he could think of no better word in any language to describe Herbert than *mensch*. The Jewish connotation of the word means a truly admirable, fine human being. Herbert was just that wonderful, or we could never have begun. I saw him again when we all went hiking in the Grünewald Forest. There were lovely gardens and parks and rivers and lakes around Berlin, so we never had to go very far to escape with my friends from the terrible events unfolding about us. But every step we took along the trail reminded me that things were no longer as they had been. Before, we'd go hiking or bicycling in groups of ten or twelve, sometimes more. The fun of it was a group that had not too many or too few. As of late, Jewish teenagers had been dropping out, and the groups you passed on the trail were noticeably smaller. The exclusively Jewish groups were gone altogether.

"We were hiking along, singing, when we heard distant voices singing the 'Horst Wessel Lied' and getting louder. We realized there were Nazis coming our way on the path in front of us, and our voices began to trail off, one by one. Even Erica's. Not Herbert's, though. His tenor voice was loud and clear and gave us the nerve to pick up our voices and sing in spite of the approaching troop. Soon the band of Hitler Youth, all natty in their uniforms, came into view, outsinging us. As they came abreast of us, the clash of our songs had my heart pumping so fast I could hardly breathe. Voice by voice, their song trailed off. So did ours, except for Herbert and Bruno harmonizing, their arms slung in comradeship around each other's shoulders. It was clear that the Nazi boys were not interested in putting up with any of our nonsense. It was surely the prelude to a confrontation. Their gaze wandered to the girls and settled on me. I thought my Jewish faith was written all over me. I was so scared. Herbert and Bruno saw where this was going and, without skipping a beat, switched right into the 'Horst Wessel Lied,' which won us instant approval. The Nazis joined the singing. And so did we, with fervor, before they marched off."

"Even you, Mom?"

"Especially me. All at once it came to me why so many people I knew were passive Nazis or did little to protest. People are more apt to stay quiet in the face of things they disapprove when they think most others do approve. It's an animal reaction. When you are frightened, you want to run with the herd, to belong to the tribe, the clan, the nation, the *Volk*, and hide in the safety of numbers. But, for the Jew, if you do that, instead of disappearing in the crowd, you stand out. Because the predator can smell your fear on you, and it encourages him. It tells him you accept his view of you as prey to his pred-

My mother's first love, Herbert Bahr, with his mother.

ator. I was paralyzed like a doe caught in headlights. Herbert rescued me. He protected me."

What Herbert and Lotte felt in their hearts for each other, their intellects confirmed. So certain were they that it wasn't long before Herbert took Lotte to meet his mother, and more than once. She adored Lotte and soon gave her blessings to the match. It had gone that far. But it wasn't that simple. Mutti had not yet told Der Alte Fritz.

Despite the ever-widening social stigma of anti-Semitism, the Wachsner house was still a magnet for many people in the Berlin of 1935. Der Alte Fritz threw a party for a few well-known American musicians who were visiting Berlin. He had met them when the New York Philharmonic came to Berlin on its 1932 European tour. Lotte's friends were always welcome at the Wachsner parties. Der Alte Fritz was fond of them all.

Ursula had long since confided in my grandfather that she was keeping company with a Lutheran pastor-in-training whose goal was to serve in Africa as a missionary. But now Bruno had proposed marriage, and she wanted Der Alte Fritz's advice and blessing before bringing him home to meet her parents. For Der Alte Fritz's part, he wanted to take stock of the young divinity student on whom Ursula had set her sights. Bruno had better be good enough for her. He told her to bring Bruno to the party.

"But if Ursula was his favorite, he thought the world of Erica, whom he called 'the new German woman.' As for Ilonka, she had become as much a part of his world as she was of ours, and he had already invited her to the party. He didn't know that Ursula would bring not one but two Lutheran divinity school students, Bruno and Herbert. I made a solemn pact with Herbert to be discreet about our feelings in front of the family. I wanted them to meet him first. Then, after they saw how wonderful he was, I would break it to the family that we were in love.

"I always thought it uncharacteristic of me not to have told them first. I knew we had knotty issues to resolve, and Papa would only want to make sure we were aware of them. I suppose I didn't want to face them that soon. I had hoped to live in a fool's paradise a little while longer.

"On the night of the party there was, as always, music. For years, Papa's exceptional chamber quartet had earned him a lot of attention in music circles. In those days, we had concerts at home every week. There was talk of performing professionally. But music was merely his avocation, his only relaxation besides philately away from his principal love of teaching, and he insisted on keeping it that way. Yet that night they performed under the gaze of professional musicians who were moved enough to take out their instruments and join in. And they all played as if they had been rehearsing together for years. Everyone was charged, swept up in the spontaneity of the Americans and the Germans who spoke the same language of music. Papa asked me to sing. I went to the piano and gave them a taste of something German, my schmaltzy rendition of 'Wie Hab' Ich Nur Leben Können

Ohne Dich,' 'How Could I Live without You?' Papa loved that song. Everyone wanted an encore, so I sang 'Night and Day' in honor of the Americans.

"The doorbell rang. I think I might have given myself away when I ran to the door. There they stood, Ursula and Bruno, and Herbert, who took my hand and broke his promise to be subtle when he held it a moment too long. Der Alte Fritz also likely noticed that we couldn't take our eyes off each other despite our best efforts to do so. We weren't going to be very good at hiding anything. I caught Papa watching us in that 'just looking at something behind you' sort of quick glance of his. Besides, you couldn't keep a secret very long from him. He was much too intuitive and could read me like a book. Paula also was a fine judge of character. She liked Bruno the moment she met him. My father, too, as you well might guess, because Bruno radiated warmth and you could see his goodness, with a touch of mischief, in his face. As for Herbert, it wasn't long before he cast his spell upon them. They were taken by his politeness and sincerity and, as the evening progressed, by his intellect and charm. But as hard as we tried to hide our affection, the more obvious it must have been to them that something exceptional had happened between us. There was, of course, the one issue.

"In the Germany of those days, there was little interfaith dialogue in the sense of ecumenism as we know it today. But when I introduced Herbert to Benny, he already knew of the rabbi of the New Reform Synagogue at Johannestrasse 16, and in no time they were talking about the great preponderance of shared beliefs in the two religions, one's love of which, Benny pointed out, is best measured by respect for the differences. We all felt very good about ourselves that night and about each other.

"Paula said later that they understood the situation right away. And Papa? As a scientist, he was much too observant. I could read his mind as well as he could mine. 'Don't say anything. Let us wait and see. New love flares up intensely and is well known to cool off just as fast.' Let us keep our heads down and wait and see. That was the Jewish way in Germany. In any case, he knew how I loved my Jewish identity, and he knew that the daughter he had raised would be free to choose as she pleased, and with his blessings, provided I had a realistic understanding of what was involved.

"As for Ursula, he advised her to show off Bruno to her parents. He was sure they would approve of him, and if they were to marry, as a man of the cloth he would offer her stability. He pointed out that life as missionaries would fill them with special purpose at a time when false idols were forcing their ideas upon the world."

Herbert and Lotte's love had to endure the growing marginalization of Jews in the years that followed, which might have crushed a less committed relationship, but their bond only grew stronger. It wasn't easy. They decided to spend some time apart in order to put to rest any question of their love and commitment, so Herbert went to Italy in the summer of 1933. He kept a little *Tagebuch*, a diary, in which he drew exquisite sketches at every stop along the way: in Jena, an old church tower; in Rudolfsberg, a palace; in Koburg, a cloister; Albrecht Durer's house in Nuremburg; the old city gate in Monheim. In Rome, he drew a likeness of himself asleep on a train station bench. There, he sketched the Colosseum and the Arch of Constantine and more.

When he returned to Berlin, he wrote a dedication to Mutti in his diary and gave it to her as a keepsake: "Could you be without me? No. You could not. If we should ever part, our souls would have already forever touched in deepest unity, and our hands clasped together in a promise. You are pure of heart, and we will grow old together."

After Mutti passed, I found this diary among the documents in the carton the girls had sent to Mutti at war's end, so many years earlier.

Mutti and Herbert now let it be known to everyone that they had found their soul mates in each other, and somehow the power of their love would show them how to fulfill it. Mops thought the world of Herbert, too. Benny was getting Mops ready for his bar mitzvah at that time. It would be a first, Mops mused, if he became a rabbi someday and had a Lutheran missionary as his own very dear brother-in-law. All that Herbert's mother wanted was for the young couple to wait until Herbert had a ministry of his own and could support a wife, so as soon as Herbert came barely in sight of his ordination, they decided the time had come for him to speak to Old Man Fritz.

"We were both optimists by nature," Mutti said, "but we were about to confront life as it is lived in the real world. The old adage 'Love conquers all' is honored more in precept than in practice.

"Paula came to the door to greet Herbert. She had always liked him. She brought him into the parlor where I was waiting. Mops was put off that he was the only one in the family who could not come in. He felt this was his business, too. Papa put a swift end to that when he shut the door behind himself and came right to the point. Herbert had all the qualities in a husband they could ever wish for me. But there were issues beyond the here and now to consider that involved our happiness together for the rest of our lives. Paula was concerned about my health in the African climate. Although it might have a deleterious effect, Papa reasoned that the marriage must not be denied on the basis of a future possibility. The one issue was, could we, in good faith, give our best to the marriage? A woman might marry outside her religion and still remain Jewish. But as the wife of a pastor, she had special duties and responsibilities to her husband's religious confession and to his congregation. Could I fulfill this with the ardor and devotion it deserved? Herbert's eyes were locked on mine, with all the love in the world in them. And in that instant we both knew the distance between us was vastly greater than our eyes. Could I leave my family in this Germany of ours, which was ours no more, any more than my father could abandon his eighty-eight-year-old mother and leave the rest of the family behind? No more than Herbert himself could desert his mother under the same heartbreaking circumstances. What we had become to each other was the best life would ever offer us. But my family, my community, my religion were under siege, and their very survival in jeopardy."

The irony of it all. If you start with the idea that Mutti didn't go to Africa with Herbert because of their different religions, and end with the idea that had she gone, he just might somehow have gotten the family out through his synod, this boggles my mind. It would have

135

Schwarzwald!

*Pages from Herbert's diary when
he traveled to Rome, 1933.*

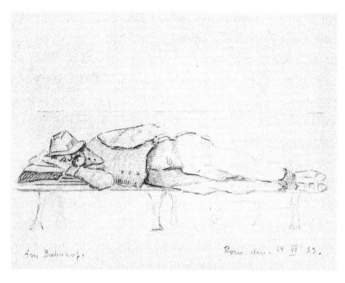

been a long stretch, in any case. Just the same, when the odds were this poor, every little possibility meant something. What mysterious force assembles such cruel dichotomies? What does it mean?

Two months later, Ursula, Bruno, and Herbert left for Africa. Mutti, Erica, and Ilonka could hardly bear to see them go. The first year apart was hard for the couple. Again, Herbert dedicated his diary for the year 1935 to Mutti and sent it to her. It reads, "My Darling Little Lotte, Take to yourself my joy, my sorrow. We spent the most sacred time together. What can we have to remember that is greater, holier, more sanctified than that which dwells within our souls. You are ever in my thoughts."

The diary is a very personal religious testament for that first year in Africa, with lovely hand drawings, Herbert's account of a new Lutheran missionary at the beginning of his calling. It, too, was among the many documents that Mutti received in the carton of things my grandfather had given to Ilonka and Erica to save for the day, God willing, when they could be passed on to her. It was clear that Lotte's thoughts of love lost were not about the man she had divorced but of Herbert. She said the only purpose Warren Meyerhoff had served in her life, as it turned out, was to bring me safely not only into the world, but into the New World.

"For that alone, I have no regrets. You are my crowning achievement."

CHAPTER 8

Rena

THE CAREER IN FILM THAT I STUMBLED INTO under the influence of Bruno began to prosper when I came home. I was getting calls for work as a bilingual production manager for projects shooting in Germany. I always spent a day or two in Berlin with Erica and in Mölln to visit Ursula and Bruno, where I continued to be received as a lost daughter found. Rena and Jochen came down from Kiel on those occasions. We truly began to enjoy knowing one another and we kept in touch regularly. I made it a point—you might say, the high point—to get together with them when an assignment took me to Europe. But not until we met in Paris, one winter in the late 1960s, did we find how deep the ties were that bound us together.

Jochen had come to Paris on a sabbatical, doing research for a thesis on nineteenth-century comparative German-French literature, and Rena, who was fluent in French, took a position teaching German in a Left Bank high school. I was hired by Kultur for a three-month assignment on a docudrama for the Stuttgart City Ballet, but the best part of any assignment in Europe was seeing my friends again. I took satisfaction that we were continuing, two decades after the end of Hitler's war, a friendship begun by our parents and grandparents many decades earlier, in the time of the Weimar Republic, long before Hitler usurped Germany. I went to Paris and stayed two weeks with them.

A memorable aspect of Rena was her laugh. If you heard it, you would understand. It was a soft but comical ripple-up-the-scale kind of laughter that drew you into its humor. Once we were in a pastry shop on their street near the Eiffel Tower. She was laughing at Jochen, the titillating sound of which compelled Jochen to laugh, although he was unaware of why he was laughing. He had gotten a funny little smear of Charlotte Russe on his nose. It wasn't just the whipped cream. It was that laughter of hers that swept me up in it and had me laughing, too. And my laughter in turn had Jochen laughing all the harder, and harder still when Rena took aim with her napkin and, with a flourish, wiped the whipped cream off his nose. Other diners, too, were caught up in the contagion without knowing, or caring, why they were laughing. Just a silly little moment, but of the sort one might remember for a lifetime. It feels good sometimes to laugh this way. I still want to laugh when I remember Rena's laugh. A sweet and loving nature and laughter come with my memories of Rena.

That year, a warm sun broke the cold Paris winter with a vivid awakening of the senses. The city was awash in sudden color. We didn't have a lot of money. It didn't matter. It was springtime in Paris. One night they, the Germans, and I, the American, counted out our francs and spent most of them on good seats at a Pinchas Zuckerman concert. The audience gave Zuckerman a five-minute standing ovation, and, in return, he gave three encores.

The Paris night was perfumed with a heady scent of spring that swept like a wave over the city. Streets were crowded with strolling boulevardiers. Celebration and renewal were in the air, and cafes were busy. Eager not to end the night, we sat in a bistro nursing a couple of drinks and talked for hours. Jochen and Rena. Rena and Jochen. They were charming as individuals, endearing as a couple. I asked them how they'd met.

"Rena grew up in Mölln," Jochen replied. "My family moved there after the war, when my father became the new *Pfarrer* of the Lutheran church."

Rena Namgalies.

"That's *pastor* in English," I said. "*Minister*, too."

"*Ja, pastor* is also used in German," Rena said, "*minister, nein.*"

"When," I asked, "am I ever going to sharpen my German if you two will only speak English with me?"

"In a few years later, when our English will be good as yours," Jochen laughed. "Rena befriended *meine Zwillingsschwester*, my twin sisters, Gisele and Christel, at school."

"They were my best friends," Rena said. "Then one day I met their brother. Jochen was only fourteen years old then. I cannot tell you, Ma-ri-an-na, how *enzückend* he was."

Jochen started to blush.

"What is the English?" she asked.

"It means 'sweet,'" I told her.

She wrinkled her nose. It was not the precise word she was looking for. She tried again. "He was *reizend*," she said emphatically.

My turn to laugh. "My mother used to call me that. It means 'adorable,' 'delightful.' In English, you could say *cute*."

"*Ja*, of course," Rena said, "I know this word, *cute*. He was adorable, delightful, and cute. He was all of these things."

141

This further embarrassed Jochen. His cheeks were red. He gave her a look. She crossed her eyes and ogled him back.

"I admit it. I am guilty," she said. "Even as a girl, I had my eyes on him. No one in Germany those days had much more than the rubble of war to clear away. My father was lucky just to find work doing manual labor. We had no money. I couldn't even afford the bus fare to school. The poverty was unrelenting, so I left as soon as I was old enough and went to Paris as an au pair. That is how I learned to speak French."

"She ran away from Mölln before I could do anything about her."

"And just what did you think you could have done about me? You were in knee pants and just starting to shave. Besides, you never even noticed me."

"Do not be so sure," Jochen said.

"I remained a few years in Paris. I worked for a wonderful family. It was a happy time for me. Afterward, I left to spend another few years learning English in London as a nanny."

"By then, I was in university," Jochen said, "and 'old enough to do something about her.' I went to London for a seminar. Gisele told me how to find her. We had not seen each other in years."

"And so our courtship began," she said. "There is a statue of Til Eulenspiegel in the Mölln town square. Legend says that if you rub his toe, your dreams will come true. So when I came home, I made a wish and rubbed his toe. And Jochen asked me to marry him."

"Works for me," I said. "I rubbed his toe and the next thing I knew I was in show business."

Jochen laughed. "My father will not stop talking about the film."

Rena and I spoke little of our families. Her father was all she had mentioned of hers. By contrast, Jochen's family was a part of my mother's German past, long before I had met them. I wanted Jochen to know how large a role his parents played as figures of my childhood. The late hour and the alcohol found us dipping into our misty memories on a night we didn't want to end.

When we'd first met in the hospital in Mölln, Jochen told me how vividly he remembered the cartons of food we sent to the Namgalies family at the end of the war, and I told them of the carton that came to us first from the girls in Berlin. But nothing was said of the contents of the carton, nor was a word said about its impact on my life. Now I wanted them to know the whole uplifting story. So I told them that I'd had no sense of family or where I came from or where I belonged until this package showed up on our doorstep.

"It was huge," I said. "I had to stand on my tiptoes to see over the top of it."

Rena wondered what the girls could have sent that needed so large a carton to contain it.

"Family history," I replied. "Old letters and records and family heirlooms and photo albums that go way back, but the first thing my mother took out of the carton was a picture of Ursula holding baby Jochen in her arms. Mutti said it had been taken in Africa when you were born. Until then, she never talked about those days. I think I only heard your names once or twice before. She really hadn't told me anything at all about her life before she came to America."

"It is a coincidence," Jochen said, "that my parents also are silent about the old days. I used to ask them about the war. I still do. My sisters, too, ask. They will only say they belonged to the 'good church.' I was only six or seven years old when we began to receive unbelievable food parcels from America, one after another. Who did we know in victorious America? Inside the first parcel was a letter and a picture of a little girl. My mother was reading this letter over and over again. You wouldn't believe how fantastic it was to get such delicacies at a time when the simplest fare was a luxury and no one had anything to eat. I tell you, it was a miracle. I asked my mother who the little girl in the picture was, and who the people were in America who knew and cared enough about us to send us such things.

"'Who would care? Indeed,' she said. 'Lotte would care. This package comes from Lotte, my old and dear friend who lives now in America. Lotte with the voice of an angel. It is Lotte who would send us such things.' Like you, that was the first time I heard my mother mention anybody from before the war. For a long time, Lotte was the only name I knew from the old days. They still don't like very much to talk about that time. Except when it comes to your mother, Ma-ri-an-na. Do you still have that picture?"

"Yes. And do you still have the picture of me? I'd love to see it."

"I, too. We will exchange them."

"Can you imagine?" Rena said. "Worlds apart and both of you had the exact experience. This is not a coincidence."

Jochen wanted to know what else it could be, if not a coincidence.

"You are right," Rena said. "Not talking about it is all too common an experience to call a coincidence. Still, *glücklicher Zufall* applies in our case."

I asked what that meant.

"Umm . . . happy discoveries," Rena replied.

"That seem to happen by chance," Jochen added. "What is the English word?"

"That would be *serendipity.*"

"Serendipity," they said, laughing.

"*Wunderbar,*" Rena said.

"Serendipity," Jochen repeated. "A word is wonderful when it means as it sounds."

"It is only right that you remember each other as babies, even if only from photographs," brooded Rena. "If not for Hitler, you would have grown up with each other. You would have played together as children. There is also another expression for this in English: *poetic justice.*"

"*Ja,*" Jochen said. "Poetic justice. And now here we all are sitting together in a bistro in Paris getting smashed."

Perhaps getting smashed that night loosened us enough to venture into our childhood reminiscences, taking us to the awkward subject of the war. We made no conscious effort to avoid that monstrous incomprehensibility, but it was latent between us, or so I sensed, just because it was left untouched, except perhaps around the edges. If we were loath to talk about it, this should have been enough for us to understand our parents' own reluctance to do the same. It was much easier to follow their example of the silence we decried in them. Considering the depth of feeling that had grown between the three of us, the unbearable insanity of what befell the Jews at the hands of the

Nazis hardly made the war our first choice of subjects to raise to the level of conversation. Still, there was the need. We wanted to know. Perhaps there were things Jochen and I might exchange besides pictures to help us both fill the gaps. So in spite of our resistance, we began to ventilate those years and break the silence with which history cloaks its violence.

Jochen and Rena were attentive. I told Jochen how much receiving the carton from his mother and Ilonka and Erica, the heroines who rescued all those precious things for Mutti, affected us. For me, they were a virtual family archive. Jochen and Rena understood what it meant for me to go from disconnection and isolation to a whole family background that I was part of. What sort of future could I have with no sense of the past? The story of the carton is something everyone should be proud of. It supercharged us, them as much in the hearing as me in the telling. It is a celebration of love and devotion and character of the women who acted imprudently out of principle over a protracted period of time in the face of grave personal danger. Their punishment would have been severe, perhaps fatal, had they been caught by an ever-alert Gestapo with the possessions of the Jews they'd kept hidden until war's end. It gladdened me to share this with Jochen and Rena, although it was a gladness born out of the evil the girls had to confront that put their loyalty to the test.

That Paris night we walked, hit a few more bistros, had more than one too many, stayed up until dawn, laughed and talked some more, and bonded and laughed until our sides hurt. We got just plain silly with laughter that magical night. Or had we begun to get sane? Because they and I, from different continents and backgrounds and experience, yet bound by very special ties, could not know that we had begun to tread the same path. All of us had the same unfinished business of the past to deal with.

The lips of people whom war afflicts so often remained silent, but that winter in Paris, Rena spoke the unspeakable and told me of the horror she was made to witness as a little girl. The agony of the child, so deep, so intimate to the soul, endowed her with eyes to see the hurt concealed beneath the surface of others. The pain I felt,

Rena recognized as her own. We both found it safe to wrest from each other hurts that until now were seldom sent on their way. It had been a process. We became the very dearest of friends. She was a virtuoso in drawing me out but was slow to tell me her own story. There was so much trauma for her and her family in Germany, and for Mutti and me in America, things that happened to us on opposite sides of the world during those self-same years of the war and the ones that followed.

She had told me nothing of her family, save the brief mention of her father. I thought that if he had he been in the Wehrmacht, this might explain her reticence.

"Not at all," she said. "Far from fighting for Hitler, he was locked away in a Nazi prison throughout the war and was freed when the war ended. You will ask why he was in prison. After the First World War, when he was still a boy, there was no work. No food. People were starving. If the monarchy you put your faith in does not make good its promises, and you cannot feed your family, is that not reason enough to try something else? Which is why millions of Germans joined the communists and later, after Hitler became chancellor, why most of them switched smoothly to the Nazis on the promise of jobs for everyone and a revived economy. The Gestapo arrested any Red who did not. Many of them were beaten to death or shot. My father was a lucky one. They merely beat him within an inch of his life and threw him in prison. Like everyone else, he never talked about what they did to him in there. It must have been harsh, you can imagine. But he was safer in a Gestapo prison than on the Russian front."

She had shared something about her father. Now she inquired about mine. I was as reluctant to talk about my father as Rena seemed to be about her mother, so I took a deep breath and gave her the short version until I ran out of air, that my parents made it to America by the skin of their teeth and I was born there just months before Pearl Harbor, and that Army Intelligence was recruiting German speakers, so my father enlisted and fought in Europe, was in the Army of Occupation in Germany, fell in love with a woman whose brother was in the Wehrmacht and was killed on the Russian front,

146

divorced Mutti, and married the German lady and brought her back to L.A., where she befriended Mutti so that she could have another woman to talk to who spoke German.

Rena was bewildered. It hadn't quite gotten through. She thought her English inadequate or that I'd lost my mind, and she needed a moment to adjust her understanding of reality to my insanity.

"The whole world is topsy-turvy. You should write a book," she said, with the full weight of a hypnotic suggestion.

If Jews still find it hard to believe that so few people in the world were moved to do all in their power to prevent mass murder of the Jews, or at least to halt it once it became clear what the Nazis were doing, there are Germans today who still agonize that the monstrous catastrophe had been unleashed by their country. When conditions are ripe, what on earth can control the impulse to destroy, programmed in the human psyche? Recently, it had been the Germans' turn, once again, to rip away the veil and hold up a mirror to remind us of our aptitude for killing and, like so many things the Germans do, do it well. I think this is what Der Alte Fritz's theory means, that to acknowledge our aptitude for violence is the first step to free choice as our resource for spiritual transformation, or, as Benny taught, *tikkun olam*.

The mood overcame me to recite a poem Mutti taught me, Der Alte Fritz's favorite, in which Heinrich Heine described his mid-nineteenth-century Germany as being not first in war but first in contemplation of the nature of mind, of the highest reach of human thought, in philosophy, art and science, and the noblest potentials of the human spirit.

Französen und Russen gehört das Land,
Das Meer gehört den Briten.
Wir aben besitzen um Luftreich Traums,
Die Herrschaft unbestritten.

The land is held by Russia and France,
The sea by the British invested.
But in the airy realm of dreams
German sway is uncontested.

"I know my Heinrich Heine, too," said Rena. "He had to move to France to speak his mind, to sound an alert for the future of Deutschland, and that was a hundred years before Hitler. 'Do not scoff,' he said, 'at those who speak of the unbelievable to come, for one day you will hear a cracking such as was never heard before in the history of the world, and then you will know that German thunder finally reached its target, for Germany will stage a performance next to which the French Revolution will seem a harmless idyll.'"

I had never heard that quote.

"More to the point," Rena said, "I am sure your grandfather must have."

Roiling up from some deep recess of my being came a child's need to be held, for out of me came a whisper of an indelible question from the past: "*Was suchst du wenn du mir so tief in die Augen schaust, Mutti?* What is it you look for in my eyes so deeply, so urgently, Mommy?"

"She was searching for something in your eyes?" Rena asked.

"Yes, always, strangely so. It's the first thing I remember. Her eyes, dark eyes, more beautiful than any I have ever seen, gazing into my eyes, searching for some link to sanity to latch onto. She could not stop apologizing for having told me she wanted to throw herself overboard from the *St. Louis*."

"It was too heavy a weight to place on a child."

I had a growing awareness that the avid attention Rena paid to anything I said about Lotte went past heartfelt sympathy and held a special significance for her. A proprietary edge crept into her voice, a certain possessive familiarity, as if she knew my mother in the easy "take for granted" way in which one might speak affectionately of one's own mother. Thus was born a new dimension between us. All my life I could only imagine how it might feel to have a sister of my own. Now the feeling swept through me. With Rena, I felt free to share what I had come to know and guess about Lotte and my family in Germany. Rena, the German Christian, and I, the American Jew, together talking about the horror and the heartache of what an insane person who achieved power had brought to both our lives.

"You were born safe in America," Rena said, "but you, too, are a victim of the war, for you are the child of a survivor."

I had always resisted conceptualizing myself that way. To be a victim is no badge of honor to display proudly like a soldier with battle ribbons across his chest. It embarrasses me, gives me a disgusting feeling, as if I aim to solicit sympathy. Is it any wonder that people do not want to talk of these things? But Rena's focus was, like my grandfather's, to let the catharsis begin. To acknowledge is to deal with. To keep silent congests the soul. All right, then. I will allow that I was a victim, as Rena observed. But, as so often is true, the wisdom one offers another applies best of all to oneself. As you see, Rena knew how to get me to talk about myself. For her to bare much about her own victimhood was another matter.

Until then, we had talked of many things, but Rena had not spoken of her mother. The day I left Paris, this changed. It was a fine Saturday. Jochen was deep in his studies, and Rena and I decided to go off on our own and stroll Paris for a last time together. Perhaps because we would soon say good-bye, we were more sensitive than usual to each other's moods. That day we glimpsed in each other those specters of tragedy from the not-so-distant past that still held sway over us.

In the vast Église du Dome, at the Tomb of Napoleon, a shrine in which one feels nothing but the glory that was France, it struck me hard that we were standing at the very spot where Hitler, victorious, once stood and defiled it by his very presence. In such a monumental space, sudden claustrophobia clutched the life out of me. I couldn't breathe. I had to get out. Precisely at this moment, there was a tug on my sleeve.

"We need to get out of here," Rena said, pulling me by the sleeve, spinning on her heels with me in tow. I had not uttered a word. She simply knew. It was uncanny. We were tuned to the same wavelength.

"Come. You have not been to Lafayette's Food Court. Let us walk there on your last day in Paris and 'have a bite.'" She grinned to lift my spirits. "You see? My English improves already when you are here."

149

We saw a group of Japanese tourists in the street, and holding her mother's hand was a child so lovely we could not take our eyes off her. We oohed and aahed and made a fuss, but beneath Rena's smile I caught a sudden flash of hidden heartbreak in her eyes. And in that moment, I saw that she knew I saw.

The Food Court at Galeries Lafayette is a fantastic international culinary array from which one has only to choose the cuisine. We both had croque monsieurs, Rena's favorite, and tea. At the table, I fell silent. I could not rid myself of the thought that I had stood in the Église du Dome in the very footprints of Hitler. Compound that discomfort with the fact that until now, the door to my memory warehouse of bits and pieces and images had opened only to take in. Now, Rena's wanting to know opened it wide to come out, too wide, too fast, perhaps, because all at once a feeling of embarrassment came over me that I had talked too much, laid myself bare. I tried to withdraw into blessed silence. Rena would not have it.

"You avert your eyes and stare elsewhere," she admonished, prodding me on like the strict teacher she was, "when you do not wish to talk."

"Do I? That's the same thing Lotte used to do. Especially when I'd ask her about before she came to America. Her eyes would glaze over. Then I knew I was not going to be able to drag anything out of her."

"Still, so is it with us," Rena said, "except when they talk about the Wachsners. How much they still miss your mother. 'Ach, what a voice,' they say. 'If only we could hear Lotte sing again. If only we could hear Lotte sing again.' I have heard wonderful voices in my life, but what must she have sounded like to rate such praise thirty years later?"

"Her voice was like no other I've heard," I said. "It had power, but it didn't have force. It is hard to explain. She could project it in a way that made it sound as if it wasn't coming from her but simply floating out of thin air. Even in the last row of the balcony."

"When Ursula speaks of your grandfather, her face comes alive. She is not often so transparent. I had not seen my mother-in-law in this light before. She was so fond of him, you know. She was happier in Lotte's house than in her own. She told me so. Some kind of usual family conflict, I think. It was your grandfather to whom she brought all her problems."

"Mutti said he was Ursula's surrogate father."

"He was more a father confessor to her. They were very close. It means so much for Ursula to get your mother's letters. She allowed me to read one. It was the most beautiful use of the German language I have ever seen. Ursula says Lotte was first in her classes all through school."

"Yes, she's a whiz in the brains department, but she doesn't have a clue about street smarts. Now, listen here, Rena, you haven't mentioned the smallest detail about your mother."

Two nuns and a class of little Catholic schoolgirls came walking jauntily down the street. We stepped aside to let them pass. A child began to skip. A nun wagged her finger. They walked on. Rena stared after them.

"Are you religious?" she asked.

"In my heart, deeply so, but not if you mean ritually. Mutti told me we were Jews and sent me to Sunday school at the Unitarian church. Denial on another level. But you were going to tell me about your mother."

"She was killed in front of my eyes when I was five years old."

I was struck dumb, thrown off balance. I tried to get my bearings. I really couldn't fully absorb what she said.

"The Soviets swept through our town of Ratzeburg and took what they wanted. They herded the females to the basement of our church where the women were raped."

"Oh, dear God, Rena."

"My mother refused. They held a rifle to her. Still she would not. They shot her in front of us as an example to the others. It is all I remember of her."

"And your father was still in prison."

"Yes, when the Russians came through our village he was still in prison. He wasn't at home to protect us. In any case, there would have been nothing he could do to save my mother from the Russians.

151

Maybe he could have said, 'Tovarich, I am a Red, just like you.' They would not have believed him. There were plenty of sudden Reds in the streets the day the Russians came through. So you see, I, too, am not a stranger to irony. We had nothing. My father took my brothers and me, and we all moved in with his mother. My real mother could not have loved us more than my grandmother did. She said that one must have courage to face what cannot be undone. I am not to be frozen in that time. I have learned how to revisit but not remain. I envy you, Ma-ri-an-na, you have your mother. I wonder what mine was like."

"This much is clear," I said. *"Sie war stark und brav."*

"Ja. She was strong and brave."

"She was a heroine."

"If only I could remember the sound of her voice. If only I could ask her, *'Was suchst du wenn du mir so tief in die Augen schaust, Mutti?* What is it you look for in my eyes so deeply, so urgently, Mommy?"

The envy ran both ways. I coveted the loving family life she had. A father who loved her, and a grandmother. She had a brother.

That last day in Paris we understood more than ever the empathy that bound us together. How different our tragedies, from inverse sides of the same war. How odd the symmetry. How ironic that ours was the same pain. I still take her grandmother's wisdom to heart and try to remember not to focus on what cannot be undone. I will not be the victim. I try to stay in the present.

That day in Paris brought us nearer and dearer to each other. No longer a stranger, I took with me, and left with Rena and Jochen, a closeness deeper than friendship.

I had been coming to Germany for so many years in search of answers that would put all that happened into a context I could try to understand. I've heard compelling theories, aside from my grand-father's, that shine a little light on mankind's cruelty. But the unspoken insight I found was not from the world of thought so much as of the heart.

On the flight home from Stuttgart, I saw those bottomless eyes of Mutti waiting for me. My heart ached to be with her and still live my own life. It was a constant battle for my independence against her needs. The few friends she made came and went. She was essentially all by herself in the world, for her, another aspect of the lasting legacy of it all. A feeling, perhaps I should say an emotional umbilical cord, connected and disconnected us in a way well beyond that which normally binds mother and daughter. We were never far apart, no matter how far away, and the sun never set that we were not in each other's thoughts.

Rena was so troubled about Mutti's health that she wrote her a beautiful letter from Paris. Mutti cherished Rena's letter. It was very special for her that the roots of her friendship had grown new branches in our generation. She had not expected "a continuum," as she put it.

"*Ihr drei haben auf Herr Hitler's Gesicht gespucken.* The three of you have spit in Herr Hitler's face."

CHAPTER 9

London

SOME YEARS LATER, I was in London working with Lady Elizabeth Longford on a dramatization of her book *Eminent Victorian Women*. My idea was to combine her book about the accomplishments of extraordinary Englishwomen during the Victorian period with the accomplishments of their contemporary American sisters. Lady Elizabeth was excited about this approach, and our collaboration began to take on the tone of a treasure hunt. Our digging about in dusty libraries revealed that these women, on both sides of the Atlantic, had known one another and were in constant touch during their lifetimes. Now Lady Elizabeth's book had taken on a whole new dimension. She took me under her wing during our long collaboration, and the time came when I told her of those icons of my youth, the Four Girls from Berlin whose hands stretched across the Holocaust to this day. She implored me, as Rena and others had, to write a book, and she constantly returned my attention to the subject in the years that followed.

"Too many cynics today in this sad old world of ours. We must herald our role models and hold them high. We need them urgently. They are the heroines."

I drove south to Kent and Dover, then to the West Country and Bath and on to York in the north and points between. I fell under the spell of the rolling green panoramas of the British countryside. I rented out my home in the hills of West Hollywood and found a wonderful Victorian at the edge of Richmond Park in the village of Sheen. I lived in England for fifteen years. How would my life be different, I mused, if Mutti had been one of the lucky passengers allowed to disembark the *St. Louis* in England? Most of the other passengers went on to the Continent, there to be caught in the Nazi web when Hitler declared war soon afterward.

Richmond Park is a vast, ancient countryside on the very steps of London's urban sprawl, the remains of the primeval forest that once was southern England. But for unobtrusive narrow roadways that now run through the park to the suburbs of Kingston, Wimbledon, Richmond, Putney, and Sheen, it is preserved much as it was hundreds of years ago when King Henry VIII declared it his royal hunting ground. Great herds of deer still roam there to this day.

Rena had been teaching junior high school English in Neustadt, a village in the Black Forest, and from London I was able to visit her more often. She, in the meanwhile, had given Jochen two children, Clivia and Fabian, and I marveled at the way Rena so gracefully blended two full-time careers as mother and teacher. When her children were infants, I held them in my arms, and I watched them grow to young adulthood. They are their parents' children.

I had also spent a month one summer with Jochen and Rena in their vacation home in a sleepy little place called Hereault in the south of France. Ursula was the first one in the family to discover this piece of heaven. Too small to be called a town or even a hamlet, it is more a rustic road crossing in the country northwest of Marseilles, not far from the university town of Montpelier. Ursula had come in ardent pursuit of her career as a painter and felt a primal connection to this pristine countryside. A certainty even crept into her that in the distant past, her family had come from here. She picked a magnificent hillside on which Bruno, for their retirement, built a house with his own hands out of stone he dug from the land.

The Namgalies family, 1985: (from left) Clivia, Rena, Fabian, and Jochen.

They furnished it with their beautiful African tribal objects. Jochen and Rena came on a visit with the kids so that *Oma und Opa,* "Grandma and Grandpa," could see how big they'd grown, and they, too, fell in love with the area. Bruno pitched in to help Jochen build his own vacation house nearby.

Fabian must have been around eight or nine years old then and Clivia, thirteen. A family outing took us to nearby Nimes, where the Roman amphitheater still sees action and the ancient aqueduct soars high above the countryside. Jochen demonstrated an adventurous spirit, and he had us walk across the top. This is not for people with acrophobia who question their balance. Rena held Clivia's hand tightly and we clung to one another, terrified, as Fabian raced ahead up the arch as agile as a gazelle along the narrow lip of the aqueduct. It was all Jochen could do to catch up with him.

"*Es ist sehr gefährlich!* This is too dangerous!" Jochen shouted as he reached out and grabbed Fabian. "*Wir sind alt geworden. Wir können das nicht aushalten.* I am getting too old to endure this."

Rena's heart was still pounding when we got down on the other side.

"I suppose boys have been doing that ever since the Romans first built this place two thousand years ago," Rena said.

"And girls, too," supposed Clivia.

Jochen gave Clivia a kiss. "But of course, girls, too."

"And more than two thousand years ago Rome invaded Gaul," continued Clivia, who still today, in many ways, is wise beyond her years.

Fabian piped in, "The Romans were in charge here for six hundred years until the Franks kicked them out around 430 A.D."

"Kicked them out?"

"It means conquered and expelled," Clivia explained.

"Just a little Americanese they heard from me," I said.

"I thought as much, Ma-ri-an-na, but do you see how brilliant my children are?"

When Clivia was a few years older, she came to London and stayed with me for her summer vacation. Drawn to the wonders of the British Museum and the Tate, she was the most impatiently inquisitive girl you could ever imagine. There was, even then, a powerful field of energy surrounding her. As a woman, she retains her same sense of living passionately in the present, of focusing all of her brilliant, wide-eyed energy on the subject at hand, ready to absorb it whole, digest it at once, and, wasting no time, move on.

It was a winter semester break when Rena came, the first of many trips she spent with me in London. As a teenage nanny in the 1950s, she had worked for a family in the nearby village of Putney. She loved to stroll in Richmond Park with the children in her care, but now she didn't remember the address, although she thought she could recognize their house. The Putney Gate is just across the park from Sheen. So on the very day of her arrival, we took a long walk and did not have to search long before she saw the house, walked right up to the door as once was her habit every day, and knocked. Perhaps twenty-five years had gone by, but the mother of the family that had been so gracious to her still lived there. It was clear from her instant greeting that she had never forgotten Rena. We were invited in for a cup of tea. The children under Rena's care had long since grown up and moved away, but the woman, now widowed, made much of their fluency in German and French, "as if they were native speakers, thanks to you." Listening to the warm and loving memories they shared, I could not help but reflect on the years of our own friendship.

We leaned into an icy, blustering wind and hurried home across the park to Sheen. I got a coal fire going and brewed some tea, and we curled up before the fireplace in a glow, chatting nonstop.

Her students were keeping her busy, as were her children. "Fabian is quiet and studious on the outside, with much going on inside. Clivia practices her piano every day. It's a Bösendorfer. No coaxing required. She is an extremely talented girl who plays with authority and style and is being urged by her teacher to pursue a professional career in music."

Both children were doing very well in school, and Jochen, as always, had his hands full with the responsibilities of school administration.

"So now you are a Londoner. *Mein Gott*, Ma-ri-an-na, I envy your . . . *Beweglichkeit*. What is the word?"

"You mean mobility?"

"*Nein.*"

"Wanderlust?"

"*Ja*, wanderlust."

"Always for you life is a new adventure."

"Like the Wandering Jew who wonders where she belongs." I heard my words tumble out with unmistakable, if not consciously intended, self-pity, which reminded me once again of the vigilance one needs to catch oneself in the act of negativity. You can well imagine that Rena had a comment or two to make about that.

"Read, then, your German history. Three thousand years ago, down came hunters and farmers from the north into what is now Deutschland. Did they belong there? If not, why not? Their blood runs in the veins of the Germans of today. Then, two thousand years ago up came the Romans from the south. Who is the German today who can say he has no Roman blood? And have you not heard of *die Volke Wanderung*? German tribes that wandered south from Germany centuries

159

later into the crumbling Roman Empire to find a warmer climate with good hunting and richer soil to better their lives. Their descendants are Italian these days. Do they not belong in Italy and to Italy? Millions of Germans, and everyone else, went to America and are today true Americans. We Germans have now a Little Istanbul in Berlin, more Turks in Prinzlauerberg than anywhere else in the world outside of Turkey, and I imagine within a few generations they will have blended their ways into the German culture. Since the dawn of time, everyone came from somewhere else. Even your American Indians originated in Siberia and from God knows where before that. My God, Ma-ri-an-na, the history of the whole human race is the history of migration. Who belongs where is just the opinion of who got there first."

"And who gets to stay the longest," I added.

"*Ja, ja,*" she said. "It is one thing to look for new hunting grounds when you cannot feed your family, but quite the opposite to be forced to go from the land you love. I always admire *die Schildkrote*. What is the English?"

"The turtle."

"The turtle lives snug in his castle, yet carries it upon his back and so is always at home wherever he goes. If only the human race was as secure in its own skin."

"Quite the little German philosopher, aren't you, Schatzi? Something tells me you have a message hiding somewhere in there for me."

"The Jews first came to Germany with the Romans. You didn't know that, did you? And they loved the Rhineland so much they stayed. No wonder. And," she went on, moving her shoulders side to side, "two thousand years later, along comes Adolf Hitler, who decides they don't belong. I think his own ancestry did not go back that far."

"The Wachsner sojourn in Germany goes back just a few centuries, as far as I can tell."

"Just? A few hundred years is time enough for some of the oldest families in Europe to make their claim, but for you it is but a 'sojourn.'"

"For the Jews, yes. Just look at the history. Jews called Spain their home for century upon century, until the Inquisition. Then they were expelled and scattered around the globe. That was more than five hundred years ago, and today their descendants still love their Spanish heritage so much they speak Spanish at home and have their own Sephardic synagogues. Something in them still belongs."

"But that is my point," she said. "They don't belong to Spain anymore. Spain belongs to them. They carry Spain inside no matter where they go."

"Der Alte Fritz was born in Bismarck's day. His father grew up during the wars Bismarck fought to unite Germany. His grandfather was a German before there was a Germany. They thought they belonged. To them, the Jews were another German tribe. Mutti said so, too. She said more Germans than not thought of the Jews that way, before Hitler came along."

"Yes, the haters are not the majority," Rena said, "but they are the ones who shout the loudest."

"Lotte once said the same thing."

"If, today, there were no Jews in the world, the world should have to reinvent them. It is not by chance that Jesus died for the sins of a world that still blames its problems on his people."

"I never heard it put just that way before."

"The churches so love him," Rena said, "they left his people to hang on the Cross. The line that blurs good and evil—it is an enigma Jochen has pondered for years. There is nothing in the official school curriculum about the Holocaust. That is why both of us teach it to our students. Have you noticed that the greatest advocate of freedom is the tyrant himself? He so adores freedom that he would possess all of it for himself alone. I think freedom is the natural condition, although people are lethargic and can be bullied into giving up their power to the leaders."

"In the States, we can change our minds every four years."

"You are proud to be an American, Ma-ri-an-na."

"We're not ashamed to wash our dirty linen in public. It may look like a weakness, but it's our greatest strength."

"Ursula always calls you 'an American girl.' Not an American, but an American girl. I think it fascinates her that her best friend from Berlin has an American daughter."

161

I had told Rena long ago how Mutti got out of Germany and the story of the voyage of the *St. Louis,* just as I had gathered it over the years and from what I read as a teenager. Rena never could forget it.

"Ma-ri-an-na, I have a favor I must ask. Would you come to my school and tell my students about the *St. Louis?*"

"You know I will. Name the time."

"It must be soon because we, too, have the wanderlust. Perhaps Jochen will be taking our tribe farther south than even *die Volke Wanderung,* all the way to Egypt. He has been offered the post of headmaster of the German school in Cairo."

"Wow. Talk about *Beweglichkeit!*"

"It is good for the children to travel outside the predestined path and live among other people and see and feel a different culture. For that alone we would go. But there is more than one good reason to go. You wouldn't believe how far the mark takes you in Cairo. At last, a break from teaching. I now will become the lady of the house, the mother who stays home and takes care of her family."

"Sounds like the same thing you've always done, minus being a school teacher."

"Ma-ri-an-na, you will come to Egypt and we will rent a house trailer and travel a route we are told is so beautiful, our eyes will not believe it. Jochen said to tell you. We will take the trip of a lifetime with you and the children."

Before I fell asleep that night, the day we spent together sent me to my journal. I didn't want to forget it. I never did take that trip in Egypt with them. Mutti fell terribly ill just then, and I came home to America to see to her care.

We got in the car the next day and drove to Stonehenge, constantly interrupting and finishing each other's sentences all the way. Rena asked whether Lotte planned to come and live with me in London. Then they could meet. I tried and tried to get her to come. I think she was ready to say yes, just to be with me, but then she wasn't well enough to travel. Besides, she really wanted to live out the rest of her days in America. In a strong sense, Mutti now belonged to America. She never forgot the sacrifice my grandfather had made to get her there, and she didn't take her citizenship lightly. She never stopped blaming herself that she got to America too late to help the rest of the family. Upon arrival, my parents thought they would fill out the required entry documents for the family and send for them. It was naive, but that was the plan. She felt responsible that it wasn't carried out. As simplistic as it was, who knows? It might have worked but for the nearly two-year delay caused by the *St. Louis*. She alone in the family had been left behind to live without them. She told herself that I was her American success story for climbing above the Holocaust.

"You have two beautiful homes now," she said. "We have come a long way from the garage."

It was always "we," remnants together, Mutti and I, no matter how far apart. I never had the heart to bring into the open what she surely must have known deep inside herself, that believing with all your heart in the ideals of America and living out the American dream are the world's most powerful medicines for restoring lost hope, but there is no antidote to "make good again" the Holocaust. All one can do is hope to artfully and productively accommodate the heartache in the beauty of the present unfolding of life.

There were few people Lotte stayed in touch with for the remainder of her life other than Ursula, Erica, and Bruno, all of whom were in Germany. Bonds that were unbreakable notwithstanding, she was firm in her resolve never to go back.

"Who will blame her that she never again wants to set foot in Europe?" Rena said.

"She vowed not to go back. I vowed to go. It was a symbolic thing. I wanted to break the psychic barrier."

Stonehenge, at that time, had no fence to keep you out. We stood in the middle like Druids and climbed the plinths and felt the embrace all about us of primal forces that assured us we belonged. It was bitter cold on that plain, and we should have had heavier coats, but we were merely invigorated for the hours we stayed and then could hardly tear ourselves away.

Rena had full recall of every moment of that mystical day in Paris, years earlier, when we told each other about our mothers.

"Ma-ri-an-na, I tell this only to you," she said, as we drove back to London. "I put myself in Lotte's shoes just to imagine how it felt."

"Oh, Rena. You've had pain enough for a dozen lifetimes standing in your own shoes. You've had enough."

"Anyone who cares about injustice should not be afraid to taste it. If everyone knew what it tastes like, they could never inflict it on others."

"Yes, they could," I said. "Memory is short. People aren't really moved to fight injustice unless they're on the receiving end. That is when they feel the outrage. Otherwise, they're more or less numb to the suffering of others, as a rule, I'm sorry to say. Not that they'd necessarily will it on somebody else. But people have a short attention span and are preoccupied with their own day-to-day situations. That sounds jaded, I know, but that is what I see with my eyes wide open."

"I suppose you are right," Rena said. "That was insensitive. I am sorry."

"Not on my account. I know what Lotte feels, and it's a blessing to know and a curse. I'd have gone to pieces if I was up against what your mother faced. It never goes away, does it? When I was staying with you and Jochen in Paris, I took a stroll along the Avenue de Suffren. I sat on a bench in the Parc du Champ de Mars across from the Eiffel Tower to enjoy the gorgeous setting. And I couldn't get the image out of my mind of Hitler standing right where I was, at that monumental symbol of France on the Seine, hands clasped behind his back, eyes gloating up at it from beneath his cap, spawning hatred, even among the French, right there in the City of Light where it was now safe for me to be. I had no time for gloom. I forced it out of my mind. I wanted to enjoy Paris with you and Jochen. But it happened again on our last day together."

"At the Tomb of Napoleon," she said. It was a mystery but not a surprise that Rena could remember a moment years ago that even at the time would have passed unnoticed by others.

"Yes, at the Tomb of Napoleon. I stared at his massive red marble tomb, but all I could see were old newsreels of Hitler standing in the very same spot."

"You remember the newsreel of the Wehrmacht marching through the Arc de Triomphe?" Rena asked. "I always think of the man weeping in the crowd at the curb along the parade route. He breaks your heart."

It had come to the point, long since, that Rena and I tuned in to the same thoughts, even if we were worlds apart. It makes you wonder whether some unknown matrix is forever being woven all about us of which we are a part but unaware. Except sometimes we perceive a corner of it—not the whole tapestry, mind you, but just enough to see that there is a design. Rena once phoned me from Germany "just to hear your voice and to tell you I had a dream about Stonehenge." I had also dreamed about the day we spent at Stonehenge. Rena said she was always in and out of conversations in her mind, and one day the thought came to her that maybe she was having them with me. So did I imagine conversations with her and wonder whether we were thinking the same conversations though continents apart. Rena understood, as much as Lotte did, why I had been consumed since childhood with their mysterious homeland that my family so adored but that had driven them out and destroyed them. When Rena left England and returned to Germany, she left much of herself behind.

One day, Lady Elizabeth invited me to lunch at her country estate in Kent. There, I met a fellow guest whose name was Joel Steinberger, an American. I remember only that we had a brief conversation before he left for Heathrow, and Lady Elizabeth's answer when I asked her about him.

"A 'nose' for stories," she said. "He is one who stirs the literary pot. He can talk with writers on their own terms." She caught my eye. "He is one of those rare birds who understands writers. And what a Rolodex!"

I could not know what a major role Joel was to play in my work or in my life until a few years later, when he became my husband.

CHAPTER 10

Rena's Class and the Voyage
of the *St. Louis*

A FEW MONTHS AFTER RENA RETURNED TO GERMANY, I went to
the Black Forest to tell her students the story of the *St. Louis*. They
were a new generation of youngsters who had been born to a resusci-
tated and prosperous Germany, long after the war. I flew to Zurich,
drove across the Rhine into Germany, and took the autobahn to
Freiburg. From there, on to the Black Forest and the hamlet of Stegen Eschbach, where Jochen and Rena had bought a lovely home in a
cluster of cottages on a hill beside a quaint little cemetery.

It was snowing, but I bundled myself against the bitter cold and
rolled down the windows. There is fresh air in other places on earth,
but nothing to rival deeply breathing the cold, alpine, perfumed winter
air of the Black Forest. And what can rival the astonishingly beautiful
vistas of bountiful old farms with their long and ancient pitched roof
barns, distant village steeples, and softly undulating green-forested
mountains all about you? This is what you see when you drive in from
Freiburg. I could not help but think of the wonderful yearly hiking
treks Lotte and Mops used to take with Der Alte Fritz through these
woods.

167

As I drove, I turned it over and over again in my mind. What did I want to say to Rena's class about the voyage of the *St. Louis*? How far back does the story go? The first Babylonian exile? Not funny. You can't be cynical and expect to improve the world. Nineteen thirty-eight is more manageable. That was the year Mutti said all illusions disappeared.

"We had not yet been ordered to surrender our radios," she said. "Just the same, Papa hid himself in a closet that Sunday in May and listened low, so that only he would hear the news, so that Paula and I would not be afraid. But we knew what was unfolding on the day of the *Anschluss*, when Hitler entered the Vienna he had known as a panhandler twenty-five years earlier. What hurt most were the hysterical crowds we could hear cheering him in the background. Papa turned off the radio and came into the parlor with an ashen face that broadcast the news he didn't want us to hear. He had always been the fixer. I had never before seen him trapped. Not since Hitler seized power in Germany had the persecution of Jews taken such open form. Now, in Austria, physical violence against Jews and humiliation in the streets were officially encouraged. He took all this as new Hitler policy. At last, Papa's blinders came off. He didn't have to say a word for us to see that he was worried that the lash of brutality in Austria would soon snap back across Germany. I think it was the first time fear for our personal safety really hit him. We did not have long to wait. On the night of November 9, 1938, came Kristallnacht, the Night of the Broken Glass, when open terror spilled into the streets of Germany."

Mutti told me my grandfather had kept his job long after other Jews were forbidden to teach, but now his time finally had come. She was in the biology department, helping him clear out his office when Max Thiel, his former student and his best, strode right in, sinister in his black SS uniform, spit-polished jackboots, and death's head insignia on his cap. Years had passed since Max had applied to my father to be his mentor and to guide him through the preparation of his doctoral thesis. Together, they had discoursed long hours in awe and reverence for the marvels of life in its myriad forms. How could such an intellectual as Max fall prey to ersatz Nazi racial policy?

"Father was, for years, his intellectual idol. But that day, we went right on packing and ignored Max as if he wasn't there. 'I would stand here and wait for you until the next ice age,' Max said, 'if I had the time, which I don't. You will please acknowledge me, now.'

"'I will acknowledge you when take your hat off in my office.'"

Max took his hat off at once. I had known him for years, but when I looked in his eyes, I saw what had not been there when we were schoolmates, an assumed mask of arrogance proper to the face of an SS man.

"'You will excuse me if I don't beg your pardon. I am not here on official business. I wanted to let you know how sorry I am for what has happened. Under the circumstances, I thought it more respectful if I came myself.'

"'Respect?' Papa asked. 'Where has your logic fled? You think you can spit us out like vomit and come in here and talk of respect? Thank you for your concern. Now if you will excuse us, this is still my office until I clear my things out of here.'

"'I can see that it was a mistake to come,' Max said. 'You should be happier than you are to know you have a friend these days in high places, after all you have done for me.' He put his cap back on and started for the door. 'Who knows?' he said. 'Sometimes one door closes and another one opens, Herr Professor.'" Then he was gone.

"A few months before I left Germany in 1939, Papa was made principal of an all-Jewish school. In no time he whipped up his student body to perform at the highest scholastic level. He thought they were a wonderful group of achievers. 'Ardent, inquisitive learners.' But he knew he was being used as a Berlin showpiece for foreigners and the foreign press, to whom the Nazis insisted the Jews were telling lies about their treatment. The regime that ruled by fear held my father hostage. And there was no escape. His students would take their brilliance to the gas chamber, along with their teacher."

Der Alte Fritz was clutching at straws, and time was running out. Following Kristallnacht was the perfect time for thieves in high places to make money from the plight of the victims. The director of immigration for Cuba made available a limited number of landing permits

169

to "persons seeking to immigrate," a euphemistic reference to Jews. Preference would be given to married couples and families.

These circumstances were very different from the ones Lotte and Herbert had faced. Now, Der Alte Fritz urgently insisted that Mutti marry Warren and leave. She had been raised to strict obedience so she knew she must obey, but she dreaded saying good-bye to her family and friends. And what about the safety of Mops? How could she leave her brother behind? Her father told her not to worry and assured her that he had made arrangements for Mops. He promised her that no matter what happened, Mops would be safe.

The marriage ceremony was performed at home in December with Benny officiating. My father sailed for Cuba the very same day. Mutti's ticket booked her on the *St. Louis*, departing for Cuba in May, six months later. She wrote to Ursula and Bruno in Africa to let them know she was getting out of Germany and would send them her new address when she had one.

The night before she sailed, the family had dinner together. They did all they could to display a positive attitude for one another, but they ate in silence. They knew that if any of them spoke, they would all break down together. After dinner, Mutti spent a while alone with each of them.

It was a woeful day when the professor, Ilonka, and Erica accompanied Lotte and the one suitcase the Nazis allowed her to take, to the Hauptbahnhoff Zoo Station, there to take the train to Hamburg. It was a good thing that the girls were there. Jews unaccompanied by Aryans, converging on Hamburg to sail, were being maligned and beaten by Nazi hooligans whom Goebbels made sure would be there to hound them until the last possible moment. Helping Jews was a dangerous game. Mutti tried to dissuade them from coming, but the girls "were not afraid." Erica was stubborn, as she always was, and Ilonka, under no circumstances, would fail to stick by Mutti to the very end because their dearest sister in the world was leaving and they could hardly bear to part. They knew they were not likely to see one another again. On the quay, Der Alte Fritz watched while the girls said good-bye. There was no way to express the million endearments that ran riot through their minds. It was time to board. My grandfather took his daughter in his arms as they bade farewell. He painted a happy picture of a Wachsner family reunion in America, when he, Ernst, Paula, and the whole extended clan would meet again. As Lotte stepped up the gangplank, Der Alte Fritz gave her a beautiful embroidered lace handkerchief that had belonged to her birth mother, Charlotte. Mutti's eyes were focused on infinity, as if far off she could still see my grandfather waving good-bye. When the *St. Louis* left its berth, he disappeared from view and from her life forever.

As I drove into Stegen Eschbach, I felt as blue, remembering these things, as I was the day Mutti told me of them, but depression was not what I wanted to project to Rena's class. Still, facts and details and such are only intellectual. I wanted them to feel what the people aboard the *St. Louis* felt.

The roads into the forest beyond Stegen Eschbach were still snowed in from a recent storm, so Rena and I took the fifteen-minute train ride to her school in the village of Neustadt.

"Class, I want to introduce Miss Ma-ri-an-na Meyerhoff. She is my best friend from America. I have told you that her mother is a survivor of the Holocaust." Rena turned to me and smiled. "They also know you come from Hollywood, California."

To the latter, I attributed the American greeting of whistle calls from the boys. Years of American occupation had had its effect upon what once was the staid demeanor of a student in a German school. The strict academic days of my grandfather were long gone. I thought, If this lapse in discipline was the influence of American culture, it wasn't going to hurt them one bit.

More whistles from the boys. The girls became annoyed by their carryings-on. With one stern look from Rena, the class quieted down.

"*Hallo. Ich bin Ma-ri-an-na Meyerhoff.* What we will cover is a part of history, but after all, this is an English class and Frau Namgalies has asked me to speak to you in English only. Yes, my mother is a survivor of the Holocaust. But I see all of us as survivors of that catastrophe.

171

Because it was so huge that everyone on Earth is still diminished in some way by it. For example, any one of us in this room today more than likely had a relative who fought in the war, perhaps even one of the twenty million who died in the war."

I asked for a show of hands. Not a hand went up. The silence was deafening. Off to a bad start, I thought. Do something, anything, but do it now. I raised my hand. Rena raised hers. Then a girl raised her hand. Another hand went up, and another, and another, until quite a few hands were raised. I realized that Rena was indeed a teacher who sent her students home with questions to ask of their fathers and grandfathers, men who fought for Hitler and, whether remorseful or nostalgic, would rather not have had to talk of it.

"My family was killed in the Holocaust. But your own kin, too, were the victims. Cousins, brothers, sisters never born who would have been sitting next to you now as classmates. Or, perhaps, the ones never born might have been us. Everyone on earth was impoverished in some way by the war."

Eyes met. A student turned and looked behind him, another stared around the room. They listened attentively, and this is the story I told them of Lotte and her fellow passengers aboard the *St. Louis*, bound for Cuba, a saga of world shame.

The ship was among the last liners to leave Germany. There were 937 passengers, harried families trying to get away before the Hitler noose tightened, a rapidly approaching reality that was soon to close off every avenue of escape from the Continent. They thought they were the lucky few. Some of the passengers, like my mother, were women and children whose husbands and fathers had already arrived in Cuba and were anticipating the imminent reunion of their families. They had already been forced to sell their homes and their possessions for a fraction of their true value. Now, what few valuables they had left went for a pittance to raise the cash they needed to pay for the extortion fees demanded for steamship passage and for the all-important Cuban landing permits that would authorize them to enter Cuba.

"On the high seas," Mutti said, "it was our first taste of freedom in years. How wonderful not to worry, not to have to look behind you. I had forgotten what it felt like to be safe. Families began to celebrate their good fortune. I would have, too, had my family been aboard. As it was, I wondered if I would ever see them again. People were opening bottles of champagne. Why not? The *St. Louis* was a luxury liner. The food and accommodations and service were world class. Soon we would be making new lives, perhaps not free from bigotry, but free from persecution. Many of us also had U.S. quota numbers, which, when called, would authorize us to go on from Cuba to America."

Coldbloodedly using extortion in front of the whole world to line their own pockets didn't seem to embarrass the authorities. After all, wasn't it familiar practice to treat this kind of refugee as fair game? So what if they had to surrender to the greed of authorities on both sides of the Atlantic who were overjoyed to take full financial advantage of their anguish? It was a blessing enough for them to arrive penniless with nothing but their lives, their families, and the clothes on their back. They would rebuild their lives again, their careers. They would persevere.

As low and heartless and cynical as the officials' crass money grubbing was, it was the least of their cruelties. When the *St. Louis* arrived in Havana, the passengers were not permitted to disembark.

Their landing permits had been invalidated by the Cuban authorities even before the *St. Louis* set sail from Hamburg. If forced to return to Germany, my mother and her fellow passengers would fall prey again to the Nazis. Not to worry. Every effort was being made to let them disembark. In a worst-case scenario, such as this, where high-profile issues of humanity were concerned, surely some country, eager to demonstrate its values as a society, would let them in. America would take them or Canada. Minimal standards of international rescue demanded it.

I wanted the students to understand that these passengers were parents with children, some their own age, families very much like their

The St. Louis.

The St. Louis *leaving Hamburg, 1939.*

Lotte at sea, 1939.

own, with one difference. As painful as it was to flee their country, their aim was to reach a place where no one was determined to murder them for that difference.

"Think how frightened and betrayed you would feel," I told them, "if you and your parents were a family on the *St. Louis*. My mother's heart was broken to realize they were thought to be so undesirable that a worldwide fuss was made over what to do with them. The 937 passengers would so easily have been absorbed into and productive members of society for any country that would take them."

I let the students know that Mutti had left behind a part of herself that remained with her family and died with them. She would hardly ever speak of the *St. Louis*. She shrugged off my questions for years. They were painful for me to ask, more so for her to answer. But she realized, as time passed, that she wanted me to know. She wanted to tell me herself of the shameful drama of the voyage of the *St. Louis* that played itself out on the world stage.

I told the students that the *St. Louis* lay at anchor in Havana Bay for a week. Mother said it was agony on board, no air, sweltering humidity, not knowing, waiting, unwanted and not belonging, their lives in the balance, while every effort to get them off the ship continued day and night. There were endless debates on what they must do to save themselves, but no one had the power to do anything. Their hopes soared and crashed at every minor rumor and tidbit of news, but it was up to the Cuban president, and his heart was unyielding. He ordered the ship out of Havana harbor.

The pockets of these racketeers masquerading as statesmen and diplomats were lined with every last penny of blood money they could suck out of the unfortunates, knowing in advance they would not deliver them their freedom. Had these families been their own, how keen then would their sense of outraged injustice have been? But in the case of Jewish refugees, the profiteers found it so easy to set aside the most cherished tenets of their own humanity.

At sunrise on the morning of June 2, my mother stood at the railing on deck as the *St. Louis* weighed anchor. The Havana Harbor Patrol was circling, warning away small craft carrying frantic husbands and fathers trying to catch a last sight of their wives and children on the crowded decks high above them, before they were gone. As the ship got underway, Mutti heard a breeze carry my father's voice from far off, "Loh-ta." She looked frantically for him. There were dozens of small craft out there with men waving their arms. Any one of them could have been him. She heard her name called out again. It was his voice, clearly. Perhaps my father was in one of those boats. She was never sure. But she was certain that he was somewhere nearby, across the chasm of light-years between her captivity and his freedom. They had no expectation that they would ever see each other again.

"Cuba betrayed us," my mother said. "They were cheating us out of our lives. Especially, parents were panicky for their children. But it never crossed my mind that the St. Louis would actually be forced to sail back to Europe. We ought not to worry. Soon, we would be off the coast of America, haven to the persecuted even before that country was born. Surely, America would let us reach out to her in such dire circumstances, as she had for millions upon millions of homeless refugees before us who now made up the American people.

"Night fell. All debates and meetings and conversations stopped. There was silence aboard the St. Louis. Every eye was fixed on the port side, where we saw the lights of Miami. There, so close, was that blessed place, built on principles, the United States of America, everybody's promised land.

"In the morning, a U.S. Coast Guard cutter appeared and circled the St. Louis. We were relieved to see the ship, come from America to watch over us, perhaps even to escort us into port. But it was only there to warn us away from American territorial waters. To be turned down by America in an emergency such as this shocked us. It brought the meaning of rejection to a new understanding of the world. We were somehow in the wrong just for trying to stay alive. Talk about not belonging. You can't imagine how low our morale, our self-esteem had been driven. We were Jews. We were undesirables, shamed in front of the whole world. I had to remind myself that the ones who had the power to put Hitler in his place and did not, encouraged him. They are the ones who should have been ashamed."

Freedom seemed as close as those lights of Miami, but pleas to Washington went unanswered. Desperate cables begged the White House just to allow the children to come ashore. Not even that. Mutti believed with all her heart that if there had been firm protests in the world against the persecution, Hitler would have backed down, as bullies will do in their cowardice. Instead, the American Coast Guard ship, proudly flying the Stars and Stripes, chased the *St. Louis* away. Nor would Canada allow the *St. Louis* to make port.

Send these, the homeless, tempest-tost to me,
I lift my lamp beside the golden door!

That lofty promise is engraved on the Statue of Liberty, our emblem to the world of safe haven in America. It touches us, for we ourselves are the "tempest-tost" and their descendents. But Lady Liberty closed her eyes the day the *St. Louis* sailed north along the coastline. Passengers wept openly on every deck. One man said he was more afraid of concentration camps than of drowning and threw himself overboard. He was rescued and did not return to the *St. Louis*.

Running low on fuel, Gustav Schroder, the heroic German captain of the *St. Louis*, refused to return the refugees to the further persecution that certainly awaited them at home. Captain Schroeder went so far as to consider putting the passengers in lifeboats and scuttling the ship. They were on the high seas when England, France, the Netherlands, and Belgium agreed to divide the refugees between them. The passengers who were granted asylum in England were to survive their ordeal. Of the passengers who were accepted on the Continent, many were destined to meet the same fate as the rest of their coreligionists. Mutti was sent to Holland and interred in Rotterdam, and then in Westerbork Detention Camp. Her introduction to the filth and squalor of camp life began with having to stand at attention with women detainees for hours on end without sanitary privileges. Her health deteriorated rapidly in the camp, and she contracted tuberculosis. Her stamina was never the same. She never got over the guilt of stealing a bunkmate's morsel of bread. I remember pointing out to her that she was starving.

"So was she," she replied.

My grandfather still had his radio. Jews were not ordered to surrender them until the following September. He heard the mocking newsmen report that Cuba and the rest of the world didn't want the Jews any more than Germany did. Few people stopped to think that the mass expulsion of citizens of any country, Jews or not, would have created an acute refugee problem for other countries to absorb so fast. When the *St. Louis* was turned away, it gave Hitler a propaganda victory at a time when he was measuring how far and at what pace the world would let him go in his war against the Jews.

But Professor Wachsner was a resourceful man. He wasn't finished. He had old, solid academic friendships in Holland—among them, people close to the royal family. Someone entered Lotte's barracks in the dead of night, rolled her up in a blanket, and smuggled her out of Westerbork. These courageous Dutchmen kept her in hiding on a farm for six months until she regained her strength. Under the nose of the authorities, they put her aboard a cargo ship bound for Cuba. Her documents were useless, and she was thrown into prison in Havana. She spoke no Spanish. The guards spoke no German. Finally, she managed to communicate to a guard that she had a husband in Cuba and gave the man the name of the coffee plantation where he worked. That is how she was reunited with my father.

Lotte fondly remembered those Dutch men and women who saved her life. They were from the town of Laren. I have photographs of them, but I never knew their names. Soon the war began and the Wehrmacht invaded Holland. Queen Wilhelmina fled to England, and the few remaining avenues of escape slammed shut. My mother has the distinction of being the only passenger aboard the *St. Louis* who made her way back to Cuba and to safety in the nick of time, just before the war began.

Lotte and Warren reunited at the coffee plantation near Havana, Cuba, 1940.

I contacted the local Dutch newspapers, asking them to publish the pictures of those heroic Dutchmen to see whether a descendant might recognize them, thinking it was a story of great human courage. I offered to pay for the space. I never heard back from them. I met with the Dutch consulate in Los Angeles. He was very cordial, but nothing could be done from Los Angeles.

Hands were waving around the classroom. Indignation summarized the students' response. It was hard for them to believe the perpetrators' cheerful willingness to perform their chilling outrage so openly, as if behaving that way was an acceptable norm. These youths had been taught to believe the civilized world didn't work that way. Some students struggled to reconcile the atrocity with parents whom they loved and who most certainly could not have done such things. It was not lost on others that there was enough guilt in the world to go all the way around.

For Rena to teach about the Holocaust gave her pupils the tools to think independently and hone their own sense of betrayed honor and justice. But what did it say about a German educational system that did not have the Holocaust in its curriculum? Where was the contrition? Why was the system not ashamed to deprive its students of the healing power of remorse? Wouldn't owning up to it and teaching new generations right from wrong be the better way to "make good again"?

Rena and I said good-bye, promising to meet on that fabulous vacation tour of Egypt we would take together, a trip that never happened because soon Mutti was to fall ill again. As for me, I planned to pack up and go home for a while. It had been ages since I had seen my mother.

CHAPTER 11

A New Direction

No sooner had I arrived back in London than Mutti called, asking me to come immediately. Benny had suffered a massive heart attack. He was asking for me. There wasn't much time. I took the next plane home and went straight to the hospital. Benny was comatose. The countdown had begun. I thought I was too late. Mutti was sitting by his bedside. Her eyes were fixed intensely on the end of a man and an epoch. I took Benny's hand, and I, too, lost myself in a kaleidoscope of images of the rabbi whose life had been so intimately bound up with my family since the imperial days of Kaiser Wilhelm.

There were longer and longer gaps in his breathing. Some power told Benny I was there, for he opened his eyes. He could not speak. I asked him to squeeze my hand if he knew who I was. Benny squeezed my hand and died. He was in his eighties. We buried his ashes in Forest Lawn Cemetery. A handful of aged worshipers, the last remnants of his congregation, attended his funeral.

> Blessed be His Holy Name,
> God lift the sun at break of day.
> And if by deeds shall I be known,
> Let good be reaped where I have sown.

His simple children's prayer is the enduring bequest of *tikkun olam*.

Mutti, too, was ailing now and constantly exhausted. I made her promise to see the doctor to get to the bottom of it. She didn't tell me she already had.

I came home in time that year to spend Independence Day with her. I had missed the Fourth during the years I lived in Europe. As a teenager, I loved being on Santa Monica Beach all day with my friends, downing countless hot dogs, chugalugging ice cold sodas, and swimming in the frigid ocean under a hot sun and a blue cloudless sky. Then at night, we would roll ourselves up all sandy and salty in our beach blankets and lie down near the pier in the still warm sand and watch the fireworks burst right above our heads. I am not ashamed to say I got a rush when the stars burst red, white, and blue.

Mutti sat on the veranda of my house on Queens Road in the hills above the Sunset Strip, miles from the beach, which offered a wonderful cityscape view framing the Pacific beyond. It was an ideal spot from which to watch the Santa Monica fireworks. No hot dogs and soda for Lotte. All she wanted was her usual coffee, pie, and the everpresent cigarette dangling from her yellowed fingertips. The Fourth of July had been etched in my memory as the first American holiday we had celebrated, at the invitation of our neighbors the McCoys, when we hardly spoke any English. They made us feel that it was our holiday, too, and that we belonged. To this day Corky and I are like brother and sister, and Corky and Sandy McCoy's children and grandchildren call me aunt. The Fourth of July has remained special ever since. It resurrected old patriotic feelings that Mutti once held for Germany, for she was born to love her country. She was a Berlinerin, and the ghosts of Berlin clung to her like a shroud. She was forever surprised that I nurtured my own attachment to the city I more than likely would have been born in, as had everyone in my line as far back as I knew.

Night fell, and the sky exploded in a shower of light. Mutti stared at the display with unblinking eyes, and what she said sounded like a conversation she had often held with herself.

"In our house, we didn't need a Hitler to make our hearts beat for Germany. Patriotism meant something to us long before we ever heard of him. America. It is unlikely that the founding fathers should all have appeared at the same time in history. They made a country that stands alone as a model for everybody. But just mention the word *patriotism* today and people mock you and say that to love your country is naive and sentimental. That is sad. With all our problems, still we have spread our wealth and ideas around the world with an open hand. Yes, in our own best interest, but what country in history has done more to help a crippled world recover?"

"Never in this world does a good deed go unpunished," I said.

"If that is so, then let the world resent us. I do not forget how hard America made it for me to get in. But we are alive because of it, and to be a citizen is for me life's highest honor. This is a very happy Fourth of July. You are home. We celebrate it together, like the first time."

I did not know that it would be the last.

My base was still in London and I flew back and forth the rest of the year, trying to keep an eye on Lotte. I came home for Christmas and took her shopping at Bullocks Wilshire. The things she liked she wouldn't let me buy for her and what I picked she said she didn't need, not even a lovely lace handkerchief. Nobody "needs" a lace handkerchief, but that had never stopped her before. She loved lace handkerchiefs. An edgy feeling crept over me.

We were waiting for an elevator when out of the blue she turned to me, alarmed, and gripped my arm and caught my eyes in that mysterious way of hers.

"What, Mommy?" I asked. She didn't answer. Just then, the elevator doors opened and we got in. I never knew whether she wanted to tell me something and had decided not to or whether a premonition or a sudden insight had come to her.

Two months later, I was sitting by her bedside in a hospice where she lay dying of leukemia and emphysema.

"Please, when you let Ursula and Erica know about me, tell them I was thinking of them."

"I won't listen to anything like that, Mutti. You're being silly."

"I am so tired, Ma-ri-an-na. You will miss the heavy afternoon traffic if you leave now. Do you think you can give your mother a little *kuss?*"

I kissed her and headed down the hall to the doctor's office. He knew that I wanted to be there when her time came. He assured me that was weeks away.

It took more than an hour on the freeway to reach Queens Road, and all I had on my mind was that *Kuss*. She had asked me for a kiss. "Could you give your mother a *Kuss?*" She had called herself "mother." Not "Lotte" or "friend," but "mother." I put my key in the lock and the phone rang. I rushed inside and made a dash for the receiver. It was the doctor calling to say that Mutti had slipped away as soon as I'd left. She was a month shy of her seventieth birthday. Mutti, Lotte, Mommy. She didn't want me to see her die.

I drove straight back to the hospice and ran to her room. I was astonished to find her beautiful dark eyes still open. In them, I saw a peace and a happiness of surrender I had never seen before. She was as serene as the girl in the photographs who started out perfectly, with everything wonderful in life to look forward to. It was comforting to think that whatever lies in store when we pass brought her repose. I regretted spending so much time away from her. If only I could have back just a small portion of it. Then I reminded myself how happy Rena would be if she had even had a moment to remember of her mother. And I realized that gratitude for the time I had with mine was a far better response to her passing than regret was. I buried Mutti's ashes at Forest Lawn Cemetery next to Benny's.

Now I had to call Erica, Ursula, and Rena to tell them about Mutti. I wasn't up to it. I was moping thusly in the dark of my room with the phone on my lap when it rang.

"Just calling to see how you are. Is everything okay?" Rena asked.

Rena had known that Mom was terminal. We'd talked about it on the phone a couple of times in the preceding weeks. Even so, her timing was uncanny. The doctor hadn't known just when Mutti would pass, but on some level, Rena knew to call. By now, it was old hat that we had some kind of odd space-time electromagnetic hook up.

"Mutti just passed."

"Ah, I am so sorry, Ma-ri-an-na."

"At least she went peacefully," I said, immediately regretting that I had said this to Rena.

"Why don't you come and stay with us in Stegen Eschbach?" she asked.

I promised I would.

Now I faced the daunting task of closing Mutti's apartment. I didn't know that what I was about to discover hidden there would redirect the purpose of my life. On the dark top shelf of her closet, unseen and unread for almost half a century, was the huge cache of old letters, documents, and photograph albums that had come in the carton the girls sent from Berlin at the end of the war.

In the old days in Germany you didn't pick up a phone to call someone. Even if he or she lived only across town, you wrote a letter. Some of the letters were written in the most exquisite handwriting in the form of Hoch Deutsch (High German) not used since the early twentieth century. Even old-time German speakers have trouble with translations from that period. Some of the letters talk of mundane daily concerns. Others give a charming still life of family dynamics. In a letter from my great-grandfather, Siegfried, dated July 1900, he wishes his son Fritz a happy birthday and offers his prediction that with his marks, he will go far in academia. What a thing, to reimagine a moment in the life of a long-gone loved one at the instant he put thought to paper. Other letters carry a jolt, like the one Mops wrote to Mutti from Nazi Berlin to tell her that on the very day of his twenty-second birthday, September 13, 1942, their parents had been "sent east."

I came across a most precious letter that had been sent by my grandfather to me on the occasion of my birth. Apparently, letters to Germany could still get through during the war. Mutti must have sent one announcing my birth. My grandfather, in the agony of his distress, answered right back from Berlin with a letter he addressed to me, dated June 9, 1941. "*Verhrte Enkeltochter*, Esteemed Granddaughter."

He had hoped, he said, to congratulate me in English on my entrance to "*Die Neue Welt*, the New World," but chose German instead to be sure he expressed himself precisely.

"You have the good fortune to burst in upon a family that has prized teaching for many generations. Perhaps you will remain in the profession of your forefathers, for the privilege of teaching is an inculcated thing. It seems in the nine months of your, until now, somewhat hidden existence, you did not give your dear parents any trouble. Continue to be good and obedient, and perhaps you will not scream as much as a certain somebody I know used to do when she was an infant. Heredity has also blessed you with musical talent on both sides of the family and you most surely have inherited a good ear. Therefore, music is also your legacy and you must nurture it." He was speaking of classical music but also spoke of Broadway tunes and quipped, "I don't know what babies do in America. Perhaps you came trotting out in the rhythm of the fox and chirping Broadway melodies."

Mutti had said he would have been crazy about Santa Monica.

"Where you are, there is freedom. Do not let anyone threaten to take it from you. You will do what you want, go where you want, and when, and no one has the right to humiliate you. Now you and I have our understanding. You know exactly what I wish for you and what I think of you and your precious future. One last time, I applaud you and your loving parents with all my heart." He ends his letter with "*Dein dich sehr schatzender Grossvater*, Your proud and most fortunate grandfather."

One last time, indeed. This was his hello and good-bye all in one, his swan song and lifetime birthday gift to me. I read his letter today and his words must suffice for all the love a grandfather could ever give me in a hundred lifetimes. Between the lines, he knew I was a grandchild he would never meet. He tried to hide the foreboding that loomed over their lives and to sound happy for Mutti's sake and for mine and still, with all sincerity, describe himself as "fortunate." The Gestapo read everything. There are some words no one is able to translate. They seem to be private family words, perhaps a secret message only Mutti could have known the meaning of. I wish she were still alive to tell me whether this is so. Mutti had said she surely knew how relieved her father was that I was born in safety, outside the clutch of the foulness that Hitler disgorged on Europe. When there was little to rejoice, it gave my grandfather satisfaction to know he had trumped the Third Reich, for a part of his flesh was now safely beyond Hitler's reach. It gave him victory to know his future was preserved in me in America, no matter what the Nazis had in store for them in Germany.

And there was Ilonka's letter to Mutti that came in the carton, the words smudged by the tears Mutti had shed when she read it, all those years ago.

> Dearest Lotte,
>
> It is a miracle that Werner has found us. I don't know how he managed this in Berlin when I can hardly find my own way home. He is helping us in every way. It is fantastic to know where to reach you. Warren shows everybody your picture with adorable baby Marianne. I am sure you will be happy to see a photo of Ursula with her baby in Tanganyika at his christening. He will soon be six years old. She has four children now, Eva is the oldest, then came Jochen, and next, the twins Gisele and Christel. Bruno is not yet back in Berlin. These things we send to you we held for you and Ernst until a better day. Thank God that day has come. I am not certain but I think I saw Ernst in the street a year or so ago. Have you heard from him? We had only to know your family to measure truth in the face of madness. Always remember how we loved them. These things we send are our requiem to Herr Professor Doctor Wachsner and Frau Wachner. Please write and tell us everything. You have never left our thoughts.

Down from the dark upper reaches of Mutti's closet and in the light of day this cache of family documents began to take on a life of its own. As years passed, I became ever more conscious, as the last surviving member of my family, that it had fallen upon me to decide what should be done with it.

Bruno died. Ursula's path was predictable. She lived on for a while, but as so often happens to the surviving mate in long marriages, she

187

passed on a few years later. Clivia called the day after her funeral. Jochen's sisters, Gisele and Eva, had taken Ursula from her beloved home in Herault in the south of France to live with them in Heidelberg where they could take care of her. She was in and out of consciousness and incoherent during the last weeks of her life. Her passing left an emptiness. I loved Ursula. She had been a living link to Mutti and everything that had gone before, which was passing into history. Now, only Erica was left of the Four Girls from Berlin. All this sent me in a long reverie about Mutti and her girlfriends and the whole weight of the epochal times they lived through.

When I was little, Mutti and Benny loved to go to Santa Monica on weekends. It was a major outing in those days, and we had to take three buses to get there. I hadn't been there in years, so I went for a sentimental walk on the Palisades and sat down to reminisce on the very bench where they used to sit and stare all day at the blue Pacific Ocean down below. Benny always wore his suit and tie to the beach. He would take his watch out of his vest pocket and check it regularly against the position of the sun, as if he had inside information from the Divine and was awaiting the coming of some giant heavenly event.

Someone called out my name. It was Joel Steinberger. Years had gone by since we'd met at Lady Longford's, but we recognized each other as if it were yesterday. He sat down and we began to talk. He was still restlessly "stirring the literary pot and moving on." "Moving on" reminded me of me. I wondered whether it wasn't a symptom of our tribe to belong everywhere and nowhere all at the same time. Perhaps this is a strength—if so, a strength gained at great cost.

I told him that my mother's best friend when they were girls growing up in Berlin had just passed away. He offered me condolences. Joel is a person who knows how to draw you out, and it wasn't long before I told him that I had come across a huge cache of old family documents from Germany that was pressing an urgency upon me as to what to do with it. This sparked his interest, more so when I told him how Mutti's girlfriends in Berlin had put their lives at risk to hide these things for her until the war was over.

"That sounds like a book," he said.

Lady Longford's words were, "Herald them, hold them high. We need them as examples. They are the heroines." And Rena had encouraged me for years. Now I heard it from a perfect stranger. All right, then. I would shout it to the rooftops. It would be my fulfillment for Mutti and Benny and my lost German family and for my faith. But how could I ever delve deeply enough? I would have to prepare.

"Sorting it all out in a book would be delving as deeply as you can," Joel said. "The book is already in you, the way a statue is in the stone." He asked me whether I'd heard of the Shoah Foundation and said they were going to videotape every Holocaust survivor they could find in the world and preserve the interviews in a permanent archive. "They need interviewers with special sensitivity. That fits you perfectly."

I applied for the job with the Shoah Foundation and got it. In the three years and Heaven only knows how many interviews that followed, I think I must have heard from them everything about the grief and the splendor of what it means to be Jewish. Joel helped me focus on my own.

Rena had been asking me to visit for a long time. Now, with the oldsters gone, she thought it was an appropriate time for us to catch up, so I took a much-needed little break and went to Stegen Eschbach. The Black Forest called up my immediate desire to take a long walk.

Rena, in robust health, with eyes and skin bright and glowing, and I were stomping through the snow. I would be happy to hear, she said, that her school was still talking about the voyage of the *St. Louis*. She was glad I was interviewing survivors of the camps for the Shoah. It was work that so urgently needed to be done, and she wanted to know everything about it.

"It's a strict format," I said. "We go to their homes with a camera crew and tape them. They can tell us whatever they wish. It's a big dam that bursts, as if no time has intervened. Their wounds are fresh. Some people cry openly. And the rule is we are not allowed to do a thing or say a word to comfort them. It isn't easy. Most of them are very old. Many have never told their story, not even to their families. They want to tell it now because they don't think they have long. There isn't a day I come home when I'm not thoroughly drained. And every single one of them is like family."

It so happened that February 14 fell while I was in Stegen Eschbach, and a gift arrived from Joel that very Valentine's Day. Rena stood by me while I opened the box. It was a wrapping within a wrapping, each successive one more beautiful than the last. Finally, inside was a silver heart-shaped pillbox set with an amethyst.

"He is a romantic," Rena said.

"He wants me to write a book."

"I have said this for years. I know you will do it. I will help with translations. I want to meet this man. You must bring Joel with you, next time."

When "next time" came, Joel escorted me to Stegen Eschbach under circumstances no one could have anticipated at the time.

He was in New York, so I stopped there on my way back from Germany, and we discovered that we couldn't stand being out of each other's sight for more than five minutes at a time, so we came home to L.A. and were married.

One day soon after, a friend called to ask if I knew a Charlotte Meyerhoff.

"Know her? Of course I do. She was my mother. Why do you ask?"

He explained that he was a member of the U.S. Holocaust Memorial Museum, which had just sent him a brochure announcing the opening of a major exhibit on the voyage of the *St. Louis*. He saw Lotte's name on the passenger list and thought I might be related. He offered to give me the brochure. It is a beautiful commemorative, and begins with a dedication to the 937 passengers whose names are listed in the opening pages. Charlotte Meyerhoff. My poor dear darling Mutti, I see your name on this list and I am there with you, and I know what it is to grieve as if no time has intervened. My dam bursts, too. It never goes away.

190

I read the brochure and I was about to put it away when I noticed a final page. I turned the leaf. It was titled "Afterword: The Search Continues. Those Whose Fate Remains Unknown."

For several years, the museum had been conducting an intense search to document the ultimate fate of all the passengers aboard the *St. Louis*. Museum executives Sarah Ogilvie and Scott Miller, who organized the exhibit, had led the search. Gradually, it took on the excitement and sleuthing of a detective story. They tracked down leads from around the world and were able to uncover what had happened to every passenger aboard the *St. Louis,* except these thirty-two whose fates still remained unknown. And on this list was the name of Charlotte Meyerhoff. The brochure asked readers to call immediately if they had any information about them. This was a Friday afternoon. I reached for the phone. It was three hours later on the East Coast and the museum had closed. I left messages. Minutes later, Scott Miller called back. He had left for the weekend but had forgotten something in his office and came back and heard my message. He was excited. He couldn't believe it. They had begun to assume that these last thirty-two people had perished in the camps, and did I really know the fate of Charlotte Meyerhoff? Was I really her daughter? What proof did I have?

"I have everything from her Social Security card to her whole family history, including her father's birth certificate. Is that proof enough?"

"But her trail ended at Westerbork," he said.

"She was there more than a year. You couldn't have known that she was smuggled out and put on a steamer back to Cuba."

"If that is so, I think she's the only passenger who made it back to Cuba before the war," he said. "This is a major discovery for us."

We were on the phone for an hour. He wanted to know everything about Lotte and my family archive and the story of her girlfriends in Berlin who rescued it and hid it until the war was over. He invited us to Washington to see the exhibit. We went immediately, and we found a picture in the exhibit of Mutti on deck waving *"Auf Wiedersehen"* when the ship sailed from Hamburg.

191

It has been said that U.S. Holocaust Museum is the most popular tourist destination in Washington, D.C. On every floor we saw the same dumbfounded expression on hundreds of faces from everywhere in America and the world, staring wide-eyed at artifacts and displays, not quite able to absorb it all, trying hard but failing to get their whole minds around the enormity of the crime. It is not an easy thing to grasp.

"Look," Joel said. He was pointing at a photograph of teenage Jewish athletes who had been expelled from German sports clubs and had formed their own Bar Kochba Sports Club in Berlin around the time of the 1936 Olympics. A large picture of Theodore Herzl hangs overhead in the background.

"The third row, boy in the middle. Isn't that your Uncle Ernst?"

My heart raced. The only reference to Mops I ever had, besides from Mutti and a few of his letters and photographs that were in the carton, were from the shoemaker. But here was a picture of Mops that came from the outside world. It was the closest feeling to the rush I'd often imagined I'd get if Mops himself turned up alive somewhere someday. Scott saw to it that I got a copy of the picture and the one of Mutti waving good-bye on the *St. Louis.*

Sarah and Scott came to Los Angeles to see my family archive and were astonished. They had never before seen anything that offered such a wide portrait of nineteenth- and twentieth-century Jewish family life in Germany. And those virtuous, truly Christian women in Berlin who rescued all this at great risk to themselves, about them Sarah and Scott said I ought to write a book.

I called to tell Rena we were coming. I was beginning to organize my thoughts for a book and had to talk with Jochen. We all had spoken of our childhoods over the years, but I needed to expand on what I knew. I wanted his memories, any little anecdote or scrap that he might have heard, any detail or trivial flash; any little morsel at all that hadn't been shared might trigger something else and help to shed light on those formative years for both of us and for this book. Between all our schedules we decided to be there in April, or May at the latest, when we could spend quality time together. I would also

Mops (second row, fifth from right, in glasses) and the Bar Kochba Sports Club in Berlin, allowed by Goebbels for propaganda purposes during the 1936 Olympics in Berlin. The club was formed after all Jewish youths were expelled from German sports clubs.

stop in Berlin to get Erica's input. We hadn't talked for quite a long time and I wanted very much to see her.

Meanwhile, something strange happened. Ten years had gone by since my father and I were last in touch, and I had always been the one to pick up a phone. But now, he came to see me. He wasn't well and wanted to put his house in order. He sat in my living room, looked about, and said that he had done the least for me, but I had made the most of myself without his help. In spite of it all, I had long since forgiven the soldier in the picture. I will always love him. I saw my father once or twice more before he died.

Joel said how nice it would have been if my father's new German Christian wife had insisted that their children be added back to the scanty Jewish population left in the world, an act of good faith to show how much she felt for him and for her murdered mother-in-law, brothers-in-law, and sister-in-law, if not for the six million others. It would be a little something for them from the heart to show contrition for the monstrous loss her people had inflicted on his and to endeavor herself to explore the vast riches of Judaism. She didn't. I don't blame her. My father probably never asked this of her. Nor do I blame him. Raised as an Orthodox Jew, he never would have gone so far as to forsake his faith, but, as is true for so many Jews, Daddy allowed his life path to lead him far from the identity that brought him so much pain. He, too, was a survivor. My half sisters and brother knew he was Jewish. He didn't go to church with them. They saw fit to bury him as a Jew. That's as far as it went. And that is how his life ricocheted as a victim of the Holocaust. I don't know whether he ever had the courage to face his trauma.

As we prepared for our trip to Germany, Joel and I talked about an approach to the book.

"After all is said and done," I said, "when it comes right down to it, I still don't get it. When they were about to tear a frightened child from the arms of a hysterical mother or beat an old woman to death who might look just like their own mother or throw a pretty girl in a gas chamber whom they might otherwise hardly dare get up the nerve to ask for a date, how could they do it?"

"That's the big question," he said. "But to me, it's more useful to focus on the fact that those wonderful girls from Berlin didn't fall for all that nonsense. How come they were immune? Where did they get the guts not to run with the pack?"

So many times I asked Joel a question that he answered with a question of his own, to prod me into talking. And he would pull the answer to my own question right out of me.

"Write that just as you said it. There is your book."

It was in this climate of interchange with Joel that I began putting words to paper.

Clivia called from Freiburg. "Aunt Ma-ri-an-na, I don't know how to tell you. Mommy asked me to call. She is very ill. A tumor. Nothing can be done." Clivia had to repeat herself three times before it got through to me.

"What do you mean, nothing can be done?"

"We have put her in a hospital for alternative medicine in Switzerland."

"But I just talked to her a few weeks ago."

"It has grown very fast. She didn't want to say anything until we were sure. She wants you to call."

"Where's your father? Where's Fabian?"

"Here in Freiburg. They're both crazed."

Clivia gave me Rena's number in Switzerland. I tried to calm myself before I called. I didn't want her to hear my panic. A whisper, still fresh in my ears, was all her waning strength would allow.

"An awful tumor. Aggressive. It is inoperable."

Those were her words. Even so, she spoke them with happiness for my calling, a continent away. There it was again, Rena's laugh, though faint now. I didn't know whether to laugh or to cry.

"*Vier Berlinerinen*, Four Girls from Berlin," she said in a tone that meant she would not live to read this book. She was expecting us to come, as planned, in March or April, to try to fill the gaps in the story of Mutti and her girlfriends whose hands reached across the Holocaust and, sixty years later, through Jochen and Rena and the children and me, to this day. She wanted to help, do research, translations. Clivia did, too, as her studies would permit. It was Rena who pointed out what I had not quite understood. She said the story of the girls was my story, too. How I wish I could tell Rena it is hers as well.

"Never mind the book. We're coming now."

"Yes, come now."

We talked a while longer, said "*Tschuss*" I don't know how many times, and were about to hang up.

"Do you remember the first time we met?" she said. "You were in the hospital."

"*Ja, meine Renchen*, yes, my little Rena, I remember it well."

As the years passed, we had often looked back at our first encounter. She, too, attributed a specialness to it, not conjured in retrospect but felt at the time. We were hard-pressed to explain it in the symbols of words. The meaning can only be known in the inaudible language of the heart. Our feelings had not yet been substantiated by shared experience, so you might say they arrived full-blown at the inception, only in time to be filled with good reasons and facts, dates, and details.

"Now I am the one in the hospital, and the time comes soon when I must say '*Wiedersehen.*'"

"Don't talk like that, Rena."

"Just to the flesh," she said. I could feel her searching for something to say to fill the lifetime of friendship her death soon would forfeit us. "In a wonderful way our lives are linked, Ma-ri-an-na. Nothing will ever change this."

"I know, Rena. Nothing could ever change it. Not ever." It was the last time in her life I heard her voice. Not the last in mine.

CHAPTER 12

"Wiedersehen," Not Good-bye

THE QUAINT LITTLE CEMETERY in Stegen Eschbach nestles lovingly against a hillside strung low with alpine cottages that pulse with life. Its solemnity is not disturbed by children at the village school who laugh and play across a narrow path. The cemetery is a living part of the everyday life of the people hereabouts. Well-tended family plots are planted with flowers, and at night candles cast their glow upon the gravestones and light the names of those interred in its soil. In the Namgalies cottage, a family grieves. Morning dawns with a glorious winter sun that mocks their despair. Atop a snowy embankment, an open grave is waiting.

At the altar of the village church stands the bier of Renate Namgalies. I came from America to see Rena one last time. Instead, I stare down the nave at her coffin. I am here, but where is Rena? I have never been in Germany when Rena was not. She was my friend. She was my sister of the spirit. Joel leads me in a dream down near the altar to Jochen's pew. Jochen is so much the private man, retiring, unassuming, yet when he enters a room it fills with his presence. Now he must endure the gaze of everyone in his most intimate moment of grief. It is hard to think of Jochen without Rena.

The Namgalies family not long before Rena's death: (from left) Fabian, Rena, Jochen, and Clivia.

The church fills with mourners, half-heard whispers, and motion flickering in shadows and sun streaming through high windows. Clivia sits beside her father. Our eyes meet, bringing tears that we try but fail to suppress. Fabian sits next to his sister. He rushed home in a stupor from the London School of Economics to be with his mother. She had not been sick very long. The end came swiftly. He wasn't prepared. No one was.

A pastor mounts the pulpit to deliver his eulogy for Rena. His voice drifts in and out of my awareness, for all I can hear is Rena's trilling laughter, and I would laugh with her through my tears if I could.

The church stands in the corner of a lovely little square. A gurgling stream runs beside it, right off the ribbon highway that you take through the forest to get there from Freiburg. I know this church. We went inside it, Rena and I, on my visit a scant year or so earlier, when we went for a walk in the forest. It is phenomenal to walk in the Black Forest. The oxygen charges you up. You feel boundless energy and your gait is as light as a feather. How robust Rena was! The forest was stunning, even more so than Mutti could ever describe. Mutti had discovered a picturesque little canyon in Griffith Park in Los Angeles where a stream runs along dark trees thick with overhanging branches, dappled in sunlight. It is a lovely place but a small compensation, for only by the widest stretch of the imagination could it be compared to the Black Forest. A wide stretch of the imagination was called for, though, because Mutti told me that if I squinted my eyes, I might see a pretend little country inn through the trees like the ones her father loved to chance upon during their hikes in the forest. They would stop for a lunch of sausages or venison, and he would order a *Mauerwein* ("wall wine"—a wine made from the grapes that grow closest to the wall) or sometimes, to slake his thirst, a local beer so wonderful as not to be imagined if you didn't live in the *Gau* (district) where it was brewed.

Rena and I walked down the hill and past the gentle little graveyard that calms you just to see it, where a year hence we would bury her.

"People here must deem death not such a terrible thing," I commented. "Look how close you keep it in your midst."

"That way, it blurs the line and the buried go right on among the living in a lot of ways, don't you think?"

"If only everyone could rest in such soil."

We passed by the old country church where today her friends and loved ones have gathered to say *Wiedersehen*. She told me it was Catholic, but services for Protestants who live in the village are also held there, for the congregation was small of late and no longer enjoyed the ministry of a full-time priest. Rena went up the steps, turned to me with a mischievous grin, and nodded toward the door.

"Sure," I said. "I'd like to see inside."

"It is probably locked," she replied, trying the handle.

The door swung open. The church was empty. I followed her in. We were alone in silent, bright space. Noble in the simplicity of its exterior, the church on the inside was rococo. Exquisite old gilt carvings were everywhere, and paintings of biblical scenes, vivid with color, graced the white walls and lofty ceilings. Over the entry was a choir loft and an ancient pipe organ, which in itself was startlingly beautiful. I blinked at the natural incandescence of the altars, so lovely that my eyes could hardly take them in, and I felt I had gotten inside of a magnificent German antique.

The church was ours to explore. To the left of the altar, a narrow white stairway soared very high above the congregation to the pastor's perch. It beckoned me to climb it like a sailor to the crow's nest. Without a religious authority in sight to bar my impulse and emboldened by Rena's adventurous spirit, I had to take this one opportunity. So up, up the creaky stairs I went. It was lonely in the tight lectern at the top. I was struck by the massive authority that a *Pfarrer* must feel to preach down about goodness from such a height. I remember the moment, for being in this space and time had somehow focused me. I had long since pieced together my mother's story, and still I felt fragmented, a mass of picture puzzle pieces, partly assembled, partly heaped in a pile. Would it take the rest of my life, continually trying to put it all back together, if I was ever to get the whole picture? Worse yet, I had a panicky suspicion that all the pieces belonged not to one puzzle, that they were jumbled together from a lot of different ones. On top of that, I might never sort them out and get it right, because some pieces were missing and others didn't belong. But that aerie was my epiphany, for I began to see the mystery as would an Egyptologist who patiently begins to reassemble a thousand shards of something into what it used to be. Down below, Rena, radiant, pointed to me and laughed that contagious laugh of hers with the musical lilt that always evoked my own laughter.

"So, the altitude is good for the attitude, *ja*?"

Her voice echoed up to me in the cavernous space. She knew.

We continued on our way into the woods along a lane by the brook and came to a long, high stack of firewood. I had to stop and stare because the woodsman had taken the time, as was the custom in these parts, not merely to stack the logs but to layer them beautifully, evenly, one on top of another, in a symmetrical herringbone pattern pleasing to the eye. Order out of chaos, was my serendipitous lesson of the day, hidden in a stack of firewood and a preacher's perch in an old country church.

Our conversation turned philosophical. It seemed so clear. Call it the oxygen. There was no need to preserve a word in my journal. I was certain I would never forget it. Today, as I sit with Joel beside Jochen and Clivia and Fabian in this very same church, I remember only that it was the absurdities of life that we talked of and the end of life.

No longer must Rena deal with the absurd in life. The pastor finishes his droning eulogy, leaving nothing in the church for me to hide behind. Nothing but the patter of my own memories. In a trance I don't know is his or mine, Jochen goes up to the altar. He stands silent at the pulpit, his eyes meeting full on the gaze of the mourners, and for a moment, I see in him the image of Bruno, many years now gone from the world, standing in his pulpit in Mölln. Jochen looks out on the congregation over the coffin of his wife. Jochen, the disciplined, bearing up. On the surface, the stoic, while underneath, by iron will, he holds together the raw edge of the vital part that was torn from him.

Now he speaks to the mourners of Rena as wife and mother, recalling memories from their long marriage. And he comes to a time in the sixties when they were students in Paris, and I realize that the laughter of Rena ringing in my ears echoes from the night she had Jochen and me and everyone else laughing in that cafe on their street near the Eiffel Tower. Just a silly little moment of the sort one remembers for a lifetime. I took a big part of her with me when I left Paris that spring.

Silence in the church draws me back to her funeral, for Jochen has finished speaking. His eulogy for Rena is over. Clivia goes up to the pulpit. In a voice that is but a whisper, yet is distinct in every pew, she chronicles highlights of her mother's life, of happy times and sad, of the epochal time of Rena's birth at the onset of Hitler's war, and of the tragic fate that befell Rena's mother in 1945 just as the war ground to a halt. Clivia speaks of that terrible event, but for me, it refreshes a favorite memory of that last day in Paris, so long ago, when Rena and I confided to each other our innermost secrets about our mothers.

Clivia comes down from the pulpit. The funeral is nearing the end. It is Fabian's turn to speak. Jochen said that when Fabian heard we were coming, even though I knew the way, he insisted, despite his grief, on taking the train to Zurich just to drive back with us and make sure we did not take a wrong turn off the autobahn on our way to the Black Forest. Fabian holds a note in his hand from which to speak, if he can. He cannot.

The mourners stand as pallbearers carry Rena's coffin down the nave and out of the church into a fading winter morning in the Black Forest. Sunlight burnishes patches of snow and keen winds blow long feathers of clouds across a lofty tree-tipped sky. On this sparkling morning, the procession assembles in the courtyard of the church for the march to the graveyard.

A woman makes her way to me through the cortege.

"You are Ma-ri-an-na from America," she says in excellent English. "My parents never stopped talking about you. I have always wanted to meet you. I am Jochen's sister, Gisele."

"Gisele from Heidelberg!" I reply. "Rena's childhood friend and the twin sister of Christel. I've always wanted to meet you, too."

"I have been here this time three days with Jochen in mourning," she said. "First Bruno passed, then Ursula, and now Rena. I am sorry we meet at such a time. Rena told me of the book you are writing. You must come to Heidelberg. My sister Eva lives there, too. She is the oldest, you know. She is also eager to meet you. She has family pictures from those days. Please spend Easter with us."

"We would like very much to spend Easter with you," I reply.

Just then, the cortege begins to move down a country path, past a gracious old farmhouse, a barn overflowing with abundance, and a meadow full of chickens standing still as if to hide in the tall grass. We come to the cemetery gate and enter.

"Nothing will change," I hear Rena say, although my eyes cannot leave her coffin.

"Dear Rena, if in a graveyard you must be, I am glad you will rest in such a lovely one."

Rena is walking beside me among her pallbearers down a path of flowered graves that conjure up thoughts of my mother's flowered grave at Forest Lawn Cemetery in Los Angeles, the Jewish section. Mutti was not reluctant to talk of the grave of her mother in Berlin. Of that, Mutti spoke longingly and often. It meant so much to her to go there as a little girl and well into her teens with her father. They took the trolley each week to tend the flowers on her mother's grave in vast Weissensee Cemetery, a hundred and more acres of monuments and gravestones and forest and flowers in Berlin. Mutti told me it was a strange and mystical place that held meaning for the living; it was not just a graveyard for the dead. It must be a custom in Germany to keep the resting places of loved ones well tended.

During the war, a high wall was built around Weissensee Cemetery and its gates padlocked. The Nazis quarantined it because Hitler said it was a place of contagious disease with which Aryans were sure to be infected. The punishment for entering was severe. The cemetery remained untended all those years, overgrown and wild with brambles. A few Jews were said to have been in hiding there during the war. How odd, I thought, that Hitler never destroyed the huge, mystical, and fantastic Jewish cemetery right in the city of Berlin.

Rena's cortege follows her casket past flowered graves. Here, a nun, there, a professor. What was the sister like in her heart, I wonder? Where, when, and what subject did the professor teach? And the graves of soldiers. We tread past a military memorial. Just a simple alpine shelter to protect from the elements, bronze plaques with the names of soldiers from these parts who gave their lives for Germany in both wars. There are far more names on the plaques than there are resting places in the graveyard. Up the rise we walk to the snowy embankment above the shelter and there gather round Rena's open grave.

The *Pfarrer* speaks his final words while Rena drowns them out, "Nothing will change." Even as her casket is lowered into the ground, nothing will change. Clivia hugs me.

"At the end, Aunt Ma-ri-an-na," she whispers, "Mommy told me to tell you she's sorry she missed you. Mommy said, 'At least Ma-ri-an-na will be at my funeral.'"

Where is Rena?

"I am here, Ma-ri-an-na, so long as you remember me."

Ladies throw bouquets into the grave. A tiny spade with a long handle rests upon a mound of fresh loamy soil, for mourners all will take part in the burial of the mortal Rena. We file past and shovel dirt onto her coffin, but I need to know the very soil of Rena's grave, so I throw in my flowers and scoop the soil up in my hand and I feel the soil as it slips through my fingers into her grave.

CHAPTER 13

The Family Namgalies

THE FAMILY GRIEVED, but they did not clutch it to themselves. In fitting tribute to Rena, they turned back to life. Jochen poured himself into his work in Zagreb as the director of the German schools in Croatia. His full commitment was nothing new. He had long since focused his life on his students.

"It is no guarantee against human savagery, but what else but education do we have?" he said.

Clivia was now in her last year of prelaw at Humboldt University, and Fabian would soon graduate from the London School of Economics. In a few days, the Namgalies family would scatter in every direction, and Joel and I would leave for Niedermarsberg and Berlin. But before we left, we had to explore the forest. The next morning, we took a long hike through beauty run rampant in every direction, and we were drawn deeper and deeper into its magic. We walked down country lanes and up mountain trails in the snow-patched forest that my grandfather had so loved to hike through, and we did not tire.

We came across a huge piece of agricultural equipment emblazoned with "Mengele," and I thought how proud of the name this company must be to still present itself that way, unashamed of what an awful reminder of butchery that name is to the world.

"We drive a Mercedes, don't we?" Joel remarked.

"That's not quite the same thing."

"Not quite, but it helps to keep things in perspective."

"You made your point," I said, "but still, we don't forget that columns of KZ slave laborers were force-marched past the eyes of the citizens of these incredibly beautiful woods and hamlets and villages of Germany."

We tramped on, hour after hour under the spell of the forest, imbibing like tonic a quality of air that lungs were meant to breathe. Every step brought us bounding back to earth with new bursts of energy that lifted our spirits. Across the mountaintop village of St. Peter, the road climbs dizzyingly to a cable-car view of the alpine forest below, dotted with handsome farmhouses, perhaps centuries old, perfect in their settings, chimney smoke bending in the wind, long steep-roofed barns laden with snow. We gaped at stunning views in every direction.

"An amateur photographer with the worst camera could not take a bad picture in the Black Forest," Joel said.

"And," I replied, "the most skillful photographer with the best equipment couldn't do it justice. There's a big part of all this still left in me."

"And no wonder," Joel said. "It's gorgeous here. The whole place looks like a Paramount Studios backdrop without the pretense. It doesn't try to reach for anything more than it is, and what it is, is unself-consciously beautiful."

We walked on air all day and could have gone on. When we turned back, it was only because we wanted to make sure we would find our way to Stegen Eschbach by nightfall.

Before we all went our separate ways, we met Jochen, Clivia, and Fabian for dinner in Freiberg. Fabian was glum, so I winked and coaxed a tentative grin out of him.

"So long as his appetite is good, and his grades, no need to worry about him" Jochen said.

I wasn't worried. I still brag about him, that I held him in my arms as an infant. I saw him grow into the fine young man that he is. Like his father, he has mystery in his nature, a mix of reticence on the surface that belies a subterranean rumbling one suspects will erupt someday in outstanding accomplishment.

Clivia arrived late at the restaurant, straight from a university lecture. How fast the years have disappeared! I was thinking of the summer vacations Clivia would spend with me in London. And Joel likes to remember the wonderful summer Clivia spent with us in Los Angeles, when the radiant girl bounded off the plane and greeted us in English with the merest accent.

"She has an incredible ear for languages," he said.

"Clivia's got a good ear, all right. She's an accomplished pianist. I mean, seriously good."

"Seriously good?"

"Yes, but Rena doesn't think she'll pursue a career in music."

"It's a crime, if she's that talented."

I should have known he would ask her to play so that he could hear it for himself.

"No piano," she declared. "I will not be a concert pianist. Instead, I will become a lawyer."

"You can be a lawyer and still play the piano," Joel successfully reasoned with the logical young Clivia. "Now pick something hard. I want to see what you can do."

"I am out of practice, so you will take what you can get."

She arranged herself at the piano like Paderewski and played a thrilling rendition of Chopin's "Revolutionary" Étude, no easy choice and which knocked us out. She slid from the bench.

"And still, I will be a lawyer."

She was interested in international law and had considered applying to an American university.

"Maybe I will pass the bar and practice in America."

During her visit, we had taken her to see UCLA, Joel's alma mater, and we stood atop Janss Steps where the view from the campus runs clear to the Pacific.

"Oh, wow," she said. "This is huge."

Now, at the Freiburg restaurant, a friend of Clivia's, an assistant law professor, dropped by our table to say hello. Jochen invited him to join us for dessert. When he heard that we were Americans, he asked about our itinerary, and the next thing we knew we were talking about the autobahn. Joel waxed eloquent about how much he enjoyed driving on it.

"This is what I call civilized rules of the road. You drive as fast as you like. You're hurtling down the road at 110 miles an hour and in your rear-view mirror you see a car coming up behind you out of nowhere, and everybody understands the rules. You yield cheerfully as matter of course. No passive-aggressive driving here. It's very efficient and courteous."

"You can get an eight-hundred-euro fine for tailgating on the autobahn," said the professor, "and equally huge fines for flipping the bird to other drivers or swearing at them. It is all caught on hidden cameras that are positioned everywhere."

"The system keeping an eye on you?"

"Exactly," said the professor.

"We are a very structured society," Fabian added.

"If you drive that fast, I will not get into a car with you," Clivia told Joel.

"I have no choice," I said. "I can't stand the way he drives. If you want to find out how fast you can get us to Berlin, then I'll do all the driving myself."

"In the seventies, a law was passed to regulate the speed limit on the autobahn," the young professor said. "There was a public outcry. Soon after, it was repealed. Everywhere we turn, we have rules for this and regulations for that. For garbage, not just a separate bin for bottles, but even for different-colored bottles. The autobahn is the last unregulated part of life we Germans have, and we have a powerful lobby to keep it that way."

"Where did you learn to speak such flawless English?" Joel asked.

"I worked a few years in New York."

"I was born in New York. How'd you like it?"

"Very much. I worked for a major law firm. Felt right at home. I was a little surprised how well they treated me."

"Why's that?" Joel asked.

"Well, you know, it was a Jewish firm," he replied, "what with my being German."

It would have distressed this principled and goodhearted young man to know how bad his comment made me feel. I have grappled with presumptions of this sort ever since I can remember, trying to put to rest the feelings they arouse. Can my protective crust, formed over issues of shame and guilt and forgiveness, so easily be bruised? It had not occurred to me that young Germans of today might feel that Jews of today have it in mind to point a finger at them and lay random blame for German crimes of the past. I think the prevalent attitude I encounter among Jews is a vigilant conciliation with the German past. There is a yen to move beyond a horror that no amount of wishing can undo. But there is the understanding that if it is only for God to forgive, then not only Jews, but everyone else, and in particular the Germans, must never forget. Because to forget is to kill the nameless millions a second time, to cause them to think their deaths meant nothing at all to us in the first place—worse yet, to open the gate to future catastrophe.

"Why would they bring you into their firm if they had a grudge against Germans?" I asked. The question seemed to pull him up short.

"I'm sure it was all on my side. They had no grudge against me. In that position, you can understand why I had such feelings."

Joel asked, "Why feel guilty for something you had no part of? Nazism happened and ended before you were born." His question jolted the professor a second time. He wrinkled his brow for a moment of thought, then forthrightly proclaimed his analysis in a light and genial voice. "Please don't take our guilt away from us."

Joel said he thought this answer would knock me off my chair. Knowing today what we do about guilt, who can find any good reason to sustain it? How can one face up to the past while mired in it? If the professor meant that Germans today need to take heed of the hell let loose in the recent past by their country in order to nurture the renewal of Germany as a democracy, that is a good and positive objective. But guilt is a poor means to that end.

"Guilt is unreliable. It's a negative emotion," Joel replied to the professor. "The longer one hangs on to guilt, the heavier a burden it becomes. Guilt is unstable. It gathers in intensity to an irresistible flashpoint of resentment that must be relieved. Beware of guilt. It must turn into anger against those in whose behalf the guilt has too long been shouldered, and in this climate, truth and reason don't count. It's worrisome to think where the 'blame' for all things wrong with the world might once again be unloaded."

"I think that is correct," Fabian observed. "If it is right to take responsibility for one's own acts, it follows that it is wrong to accept blame for the acts of others."

"Yes, we didn't do it," Clivia said. "Still, there is the sense of national responsibility."

"We Germans have always been an enigma, even to ourselves," the assistant professor said. "But Germany did it. For our own sake, it will never be something we no longer have to feel guilty about. It is in this context that I say, 'Please do not take our guilt away.'"

"Nothing in human behavior is unfamiliar," Clivia sighed, with a shake of her head and the wisdom of a soul older than hers. "The whole human race has the potential for violence. Guilt is not dependable, but I am told that love is, and we must find it in ourselves. If that is not enough, we are doomed. It is all we have to protect us from ourselves."

Jochen's face remained stolid. His eyes betrayed his pride.

"Well spoken," he said. "Seldom do we recognize the dark face in the mirror as our own."

As we left the restaurant, Clivia put her arm through mine. "We need a girls' night out. Mommy had a favorite film she liked so much, she saw it a second time and took me with her. She planned on asking you to see it with her a third time." Her voice trailed off. "Before you leave, we will see it together. It's called *Nirgund Wo Nirgund Wann in Afrika*."

Clivia and I had our "girls' night out." We went to see the film she and Rena were so taken with, *Nowhere in Africa*. Africa, the continent of Jochen's birth, beloved by the Namgalies family for the years they'd spent there as missionaries, and Egypt, where Clivia and Fabian had lived during so many of their formative years.

In the film, Africa is the refuge of a German-Jewish lawyer and his family fleeing death at the hands of the Nazis. Severed from their sophisticated upper-middle-class German identity, with every cultural vestige of their former existence shorn from them, the family manages to find a haven scratching out a meager existence on a remote farm in the African wilderness. At war's end, they are torn by whether they should accept an invitation to return to Germany and the restoration of their adored former identity and standard of life, or remain on the continent that had entrenched itself in their souls. I know that Rena wanted to watch this film with me as an expression of her love. Clivia did, too, and I love them for it.

CHAPTER 14

An Interview with Jochen

CLIVIA RETURNED TO HER STUDIES. Jochen and Fabian went to an isolated cabin high up in the snowy mountains to spend a few father-and-son days to pull themselves back together again before leaving.

"You have questions to ask me for your book," Jochen said. "Who knows how long it will be before we will see each other again? Why don't you come up to the mountains to visit a last time? It is just a little detour. Then you can be on your way to Berlin."

We were glad Jochen asked us to come. We would not have wanted to intrude on his mourning. We rose early the next morning and drove up into the forest. Joel was behind the wheel. The sun broke rhythmically through waving trees, stinging my eyes with too much brightness, too much color. I closed my eyes to no avail, for through my lids the sun kept tapping out intermittent mesmerizing flashes of light, suspending me in reverie between sleep and wakefulness. I loved this place. But it is an American thing to love one's roots. American nationality, I mused, is a very special and unique phenomenon in the world. In America, but for Native Americans, all of our forebears hailed from somewhere else. And for all the grief that brought my parents to America, it translates into my good fortune to

213

be born an American. In this hypnotic moment of clarity, I knew where I belonged.

We reached the area of Jochen's cabin, but there was no way to locate it by ourselves without first being shown the way through the snow, so Jochen had designated that we meet at an inn that was relatively easy to find. There, we were to phone him and he would drive down and lead us the rest of the way. We followed him up a steep and slippery road that defied the law of gravity, climbing at an odd and unbalancing angle that made the car seem ready to tip over and tumble backward, rear end first, down the mountainside. Soon we came to the cabin, hoary with age and rooted in the ground as firm and strong as the oak that was hewn to build it. We got out of our cars, and Jochen pointed above the front door. Hanging there was a primitive wooden plaque, carved with the inscription "CMB 2002."

"Do you know what that means?" he asked. "'CMB' stands for Casper, Melchior, and Balthazar, the Three Holy Kings. Perhaps they are more familiar to you as the Three Wise Men, or Magi. The ancient Hebrews knew them as astrologers and interpreters of dreams who foretold events. It is an old custom each year to put up the new date on New Year's Eve. In pre-Christian times there was a ceremony involving the oak tree."

"This reminds me of when I was in the army stationed in Japan years ago," Joel said. "I saw a farmhouse under construction in the countryside outside Tokyo. A bow and arrow was fastened to the thatched rooftop to bless the house with good hunting and bountiful harvests. I still have the film I took of it. Perhaps this is the Teutonic equivalent, a kindred symbol from Jungian depths that springs from the universal need to invoke the protection of a force greater than ourselves. Like a mezuzah."

Doorways were low inside the stout rustic hut, as if indeed built by Druids of old. A worn short flight of narrow steps beckoned to a row of bunks that invited you to hibernate for the winter. Fabian had come down with a bad cold; he excused himself and went back to bed. We sat at a table in a dark little room, pierced through a window by sharp white daylight reflected off snowfields and pines as far as the eye could see. It was warm and cozy, and I was overcome with a sense of timelessness and security in this strange and mysterious space. I had questions, but most of all I wanted Jochen to meander, anything he might remember that came into his head about his parents when he was a child, any tidbit he might have heard from Ursula and Bruno about Mutti and the girls in Berlin before the war.

"You know, I first heard of your mother when those food parcels from America started coming after the war. I remember the chocolate most of all. There was no food and people were starving, so the name 'Lotte' became synonymous with survival. I never forgot this. My parents always referred to her voice. They missed hearing her sing. From the way they talked so much about it, I took it for granted she must have had a great talent. I knew she was a friend of theirs in Berlin before the war, but nothing was ever said about Lotte being Jewish. Mother mentioned Erica infrequently. I can't remember hearing the name of Ilonka Von Patti, but, you know, in general, they were very closemouthed and had little to say about the Hitler years. I was never satisfied with it."

"Me, neither," I said. "No one wanted to talk to their children about it."

"You know, my parents left Germany long before the war began, to become missionaries in Africa."

"I know. They left in 1935. Do you remember anything from Africa?"

"Well, it is earlier than I can remember, but you know, the war had just begun. Tanganyika was controlled by the British, so all German Nationals were rounded up as enemy aliens and put in an internment camp. That's where I was born. We waited a year for a prisoner exchange before we were sent home. I think it was in 1941. We moved in with my grandparents who lived in Soldien, a little village outside Berlin. I remember the flags. The blood-red flags. I'll tell you, they really moved me. I loved the flags. The swastika was designed to reach you on an emotional level."

"I know what you mean. I saw Leni Reifenstahl's *Triumph of the Will*. You despise everything about the Nazis, and yet the film rouses you on a visceral level. You want to stand up and cheer. No thinking necessary."

"Especially, a child would fall for it. But hardly just children. The day I was born, mother wrote in her diary that she was proud I came into the world at a time when Germany would be the greatest power on earth. But when Germany was defeated, something happened that I'll never forget. I was five or six, and I found a little red flag with the black swastika and I hung it on a flagpole. God help me, I had no idea what it really stood for. In no time, the *Polizei* came and took it down and burned it. They told me the flag was evil. I was to be punished for this. I didn't understand. I was confused. How can a child understand that what had been taught to be noble and good now was evil? I did something wrong and nobody would tell me what it was. I think that is why I grew up asking questions. My sisters, too. My parents would not discuss it. Somehow, I got the idea they didn't want to talk about things done in the name of the flag. What things? In school, also no explanation. Something else happened that same summer after the war. The Swiss offered a few German children two weeks' vacation at a summer camp in the Alps. We were among the lucky ones who were chosen to go. We were so excited, but when we got there, the Swiss children would have nothing to do with us. Talk about feeling guilt. They blamed us children for the war. I never forgot how it felt to be despised."

"What did you hear about Jews when you were growing up?"

"From the people around us, nothing at all. Just one little thing that sticks in my mind I will mention only because you ask. My grandparents said the good tickets to concerts were always gone because the Jews in Berlin bought them first, but I didn't take the remark as anti-Semitic. I just wondered whether Jews loved good music more than they did. I wish I had asked them why they didn't get to the box office first."

This was an old pattern. I had read that eighteenth-century travelers through the Royal Prussian states noted that the Jews they encountered in Berlin loved the theater above all else and took up most of the seats.

216

"Aside from this," he continued, "I never heard anything even remotely anti-Semitic. I was ten years old before I heard that most churches, Catholic and Protestant, were pro-Nazi. I didn't believe it. So I asked my father where he stood in the thirties when Hitler first came to power. Mother, too. 'We belonged to the Good Church' is all they would say. By that, they meant the Clergy Emergency League, the resistance movement of the Professing Church. Martin Neimohler paid with his life for that."

"Why wasn't that a good-enough answer?" Joel asked.

"I'm not sure. I understood that they would rather not have talked about it at all, just as everybody else did not. But it bothered me. I thought their moral outrage at what happened should have out-weighed the desire to keep silent.

"There wasn't a word in the textbooks about the Holocaust. But in high school, we were given a homework assignment. We had to ask our parents what they did during the war. Other students came back with a report. I was the only student in class with nothing to say. All it did was make me more curious. The only time my mother ever said anything about Hitler was that his hypnotic blue eyes fascinated her. I don't know how helpful this is. I wish I knew more."

The shadows of pines on glistening snow grew longer, reminding us that we needed to get moving if we were going to find our way back to the road to Stegen Eschbach before dark. When we left, I reminded Jochen that Rena always said that when he retired, they intended to come to California for a long visit with me. I told him we fully expected him to come.

In the morning, before we left the Black Forest, we drove to Bodensee, as it is known on the German side, and Lake Constance on the Swiss. When we reached the border, spit-and-polish Swiss guards, giants in splendid uniforms, stopped us to examine our *Ausweisse*, before letting us cross. It's so easy today to cross this border. During the war, though, Jews fleeing from their murderers mistakenly thought such a crossing would mean the difference between life and death. But they were caught by the Swiss and sent back to the Nazis and certain death. On the other hand, German soldiers who deserted their posts and made it to Switzerland were given political asylum for the duration of the war.

We sped north on the autobahn to Westphalia and my father's hometown of Niedermarsburg, Joel at the wheel.

"Jochen said they returned to Berlin in 1941," Joel said. "I thought you told me the Namgalies came back in 1945 when the war was over."

"That's what Lotte always thought. That's what she told me."

Driving in intermittent rain and sunshine through the rolling green Westphalian countryside, Joel wanted to lift my spirits. He likes to be funny, and he gaped exaggeratedly and blinked his eyes.

"There's something wrong with my eyes," he said. "I don't believe what I see. Wherever you turn, it's too beautiful to believe. No, really, I'm serious."

Daddy used to talk about Westphalia. After the war, he often went back to Niedermarsberg to visit his father's grave and to tramp in the mountains and forests he had loved as a boy. It's a place I always meant to visit. I thought that maybe we could find the family home where his mother, sister, and brothers had lived before they were "sent east." I had an old address. More than sixty years had passed since then. Even so, I wondered whether there might be an old villager who would remember the Jewish neighbors who had been plucked from their midst.

In the center of town is an inn where we stayed the night. A few elderly couples were in the dining room when we went to get a bite. I didn't want to intrude upon them at their table, but Joel insisted that I ask.

"Who knows? We might just get lucky."

But none of them remembered a family named Meyerhoff.

We found the old address. The house had been refurbished long ago as a heating appliance store. The owner welcomed us. He knew the name Meyerhoff and told us we were now standing in what had formerly been their living room. In the backyard we noticed a fence identical to the one in a photograph of the Meyerhoff family taken in 1935. It felt like classic déjà vu to see something still existing on

218

the ground that we could recognize from an old photograph I had looked at all my life.

In the morning, we asked the innkeeper whether he could tell us where the old Judischer Friedhof, Jewish Cemetery, was. He knew only that it was nearby. We went to see the Burgermeister, who riffled through a box of old keys in the bottom of his desk and managed to come up with the one marked "Judischer Friedhof." We walked through Marsberg and found it to be a very pretty town. We crossed a gushing stream and walked along a rising road beside a lovely park. Soon we found ourselves on a handsome street of impressive homes. As the hillock rose, there to the side of the road, in this unlikely setting, the small, sweet, still noble Jewish cemetery greeted us. On a stone gatepost, a memorial plaque proclaimed that the city of Marsberg had placed it there on November 9, 1988, the fiftieth anniversary of the Night of the Broken Glass, Kristallnacht, November 9, 1938, in memory of the fallen and murdered of its Jewish citizens. That dreadful night, not only synagogues but Jewish homes and shops were destroyed, and many Jewish cemeteries throughout the Reich were broken into and vandalized.

A heavy lock and chain secured the gates, and it took a little finesse to get the key to twist in the lock. It is not an oft-visited place. The cemetery was intact, though some stones no longer stood upright, and the grounds were overgrown with weeds. We began to search for the gravestone of my father's father, Cantor Ludwig Meyerhoff, and when we found it, we were stunned to see two little stones laid upon it, as if the grave had recently been visited by family members. It is an old Jewish custom to place stones on a tombstone when you visit. They send down a direct signal to the dead that someone remembers. But the last family member who had come here was my father, ten or twelve years before. Considering the wind, the rain, and the snow in all those years, we found it remarkable, if not implausible, that the stones still sat where he put them so long ago. Or if someone else put them there, who? I'm sure there is a logical answer to this, if we knew it. In the meantime, we took it as a sign from Providence of Jewish continuity.

CHAPTER 15

An Interview with Erica

EARLY THE NEXT MORNING, we packed up and left for Berlin. Erica was expecting us. She was in her late eighties now and was not well. I knew, more than likely, that this was the last time I would ever see her, the last of *der Vier Freundinen aus Berlin*. I had phoned her from Los Angeles and found that she had lost her wonderful command of English. We spoke only German thereafter. The translations stretched my skills to the limit.

"Call me when you get here," she said. "I am waiting for you."

As we drove, I said to Joel that by now, Erica must have told me everything she knew, but it would never be enough.

"What would be enough?" Joel asked."

"Just as they went to their deaths, they had their eyes opened to the truth about this world. No one was going to show up at the last moment to save them. What a time to be disencumbered of your ideals, as you surrender your life, your last moment here on earth. Knowing that as far as the rest of the world was concerned, you were garbage, not worth bothering with at all. No righteous outrage, no worldwide protests. What a heartbreaking thing to have to know as you go to be gassed."

"Cut it out, Marianne. That's bizarre."

"Yes, it is. It hurts me to think of it, too. But bizarre is child's play next to the horror it really was. It bothers me how much it would have meant for them to know their deaths surely did matter to someone. If that someone could have been me, that would be enough. Anything I can imagine is not enough."

"Put that in your book."

The sky was overcast when we reached Berlin. I had arranged for what I assumed was a room in die Mitte, the Berlin City Center in the old GDR Sector, East Berlin. What we got was a fantastic suite in a new building in this very happening part of Berlin. It turned out that Rosenthalerstrasse, the address of my uncle's shirt factory, was just a street away, although where it once stood is still an empty lot. New buildings were under construction everywhere in this once communist zone, and huge cranes crowded the skyline. More than ten years had passed since the Wall came down. What took them so long?

We settled in, turned on the television, and got the news, which fascinated Joel, who could watch it for hours.

"I get a better idea here of world news, and I don't even know what they're talking about."

I called Erica.

"I am nursing a terrible cold. Come Thursday," she said. "I cannot wait longer to see you. Then I will meet Joel and see what you have got yourself into."

She hadn't lost her sense of humor any more than she had lost her old anger, as I was to find out. Thursday was four days hence. We had a Berlin agenda that would take up our time. All my life I had wanted to visit my grandmother's grave in Weissensee Cemetery. It was open, now that the Wall had come down, and just a fifteen-minute drive away. If her gravestone still existed, I would be the first and only person in more than sixty years, the last of my family remaining on earth, to go there and say Kaddish for her. I also wanted to go to Johannestrasse 16, the site of the long-ago-destroyed New Reform Synagogue where Rabbi Benny had ministered to my family. I knew it was a vacant lot now, but I had to see it.

We were told that German military records are kept in Potsdam, an afternoon's drive from Berlin. There, we would try to track down my grandfather's military history.

Joel wanted to see Walther Rathenau's home in the Grünewald. He was the German munitions minister during World War I whose heroic ingenuity miraculously kept the German military supplied well beyond the time when essential war materials were sure to run out. He became foreign minister of Germany after the war. We stopped at the intersection where he had been assassinated in 1921 by FreiKorps extremists because he was Jewish.

We would also eat at Kempinski's on Kurfurstendamm and shop at Ka De We. Of course, we would attend Der Berlin Philharmoniker and then see Erica before going on to Heidelberg and Gisele.

We went to Weissensee Cemetery in the morning. It is a hundred and more moody acres of forest that dwarf huge mausoleums and tombs and history. We entered the cemetery office and asked the attendant, a young German wearing a yarmulke, how we could find the 1915 gravesite of my grandmother. He went to a computer and, in a moment, came back with a printout of the original handwritten death record showing the location of her plot. Even then, it took a bit of searching through this vast place. There was the tomb of Adolf Jandorf, the founder of Ka De We, and there, the tomb of the great German philosopher Hermann Cohen.

We passed the mausoleum of Berthold Kempinski and many others before we came upon the grave of my grandmother. This is no small gravestone but a tall slab of black marble. What surprised us was its condition. Polished and shiny, it truly could not have looked more newly minted than if it had been placed there yesterday. Once again, I experienced the eerie feeling of déjà vu at a German gravesite of my antecedents, standing one foot in the twenty-first century, the other in 1915 when the young soldier Fritz Wachsner mourned at this spot with a whole family for the young wife who had died in giving birth to my mother. My mind ran to the fantasy of Fritz Wachsner that day imagining a future, nearly a hundred years hence, when an American granddaughter of his would be standing right there next to him, with the terrible knowledge of what had transpired in the intervening years. He might have wanted to be an army deserter and to go to the grave with his wife if he had known. There once was a flower garden on this grave, but now, thick roots surround the pristine stone, making it hard to navigate.

Cemeteries evidence the end of life. They are a place of death, but Weissensee is very special. It exudes permanence. It was here before Hitler and is here still. It has the endurance of a people that wills to live. Weissensee was the first place in Germany where Jews held religious services and again worshipped openly as Jews when the war ended. Urns of ashes from the death camps have since been interred here. I had never before been in a cemetery I didn't want to leave. Go there yourself and you will feel its holiness. Lanes through the cemetery are well trodden by visitors, and, judging by their numbers, by no means are Jews the majority. People had the same dumbfounded expression on their faces that I saw at the Holocaust Museum in Washington, D.C., eyes staring wide in wonderment, in the quietude of this immense testimony of a people once so vital in the life of the nation, trying but not quite able to get hold of the enormity of the disaster that befell them. It is no easy thing to grasp the ungraspable.

That night at the Berlin Philharmonic, we found ourselves among music lovers dressed the way we like to see an audience for a night of music, and not a pair of sneakers in the crowd. The hall is a masterpiece of acoustics, with tiers that surround the orchestra, and every seat is choice, seemingly perched right above and in close proximity to the musicians. It was a fantastic performance of Johann Sebastian Bach's *St. Matthew Passion*, and many people in the audience were following the libretto with the score in their hands. A long ovation followed.

We went to Potsdam on a cold and blustery morning. Both of us love to walk in the cold, but this was different. We got out of the car at Wansee and got right back in for fear of turning into icicles because of the wind chill factor. Wansee was not new to either of us.

"This is my second try at frostbite in this icebox," Joel said. "We have to come when it's warm. It's gorgeous here in the fall."

In Potsdam, we found the military records office closed. We thought, at the time, that the record of every German soldier was there, from the time German military records were first kept. Records of the thousands upon thousands of Jewish veterans who served their country in World War I had not been purged by the Nazis. It boggled my mind to think that their records lie in repose together in the same files as those of SS and Wehrmacht veterans of World War II. Who belongs where? How will future historians who research these files know the difference? Or will it no longer matter that these soldiers, but for time and space, are unwilling comrades-in-arms, stuck together for eternity?

We drove to Steglitz, a Berlin neighborhood where my great-grandmother Fanny, as well as Joseph Goebbels, had lived. A small square is tucked a street away from the main road. On that square stands a memorial called the Spiegelwand, a huge wall of steel polished to a mirror and engraved with the names of the Jewish Berliners from the neighborhood who had been deported. During the planning of the monument, fierce aesthetic opposition broke out among the local officials of Steglitz, but it was *Gleichschaltung* revisited, another kneejerk reaction to make less of what had happened to the Jews who once lived here. What kind of *Wiedergutmachen* is that? What does it portend for the future? Yet the beautiful memorial was built. There it stands to commemorate the victims. One day, perhaps everyone of good faith will stand there with heads bowed and honor themselves.

We went to Alte Hamburgerstrasse and stood where the Jewish Old People's Home once was. Adjacent is an open space that had been the oldest Jewish cemetery in Berlin until it was razed by the Nazis. Moses Mendelssohn was buried there. Now a replica of his stone has been placed in that spot. This is where the Jews were brought and rounded up. Then each batch, within the hour, was taken to the Bahnhoff for transport east. A bronze memorial stands there, a mournful tableau of men, women, and children about to meet that fate, who stare at you with eyes that challenge you to remember them. Little stones have been placed there by visitors. It is comforting that others come here and the innocents are not forgotten. Words are one thing, but each little pebble is a personal, anonymous act of individual emotion and connection and Jewishness, most touchingly so when Christian hearts come by to place a stone.

Joel wanted our picture taken together here. Coming down the street were three huge, brutal-looking bruisers who looked like what you might think of as typical SS men. They stopped and stared at us, or were they staring at the memorial? Hoping for the best, Joel asked one of them if he would take our picture. Most sincerely and graciously, he eagerly took our picture, and he took another one, saying, "Just to make sure." Plenty of eye contact from all three, communicating heartfelt feelings more than words ever could. Then they were on their way. I took this as a reminder not to generalize and come to conclusions about people too quickly. It was a lovely, touching moment.

Thursday, I took the wheel and drove the basic route to Erica's, down Friedrichstrasse, turning right on Unter Den Linden, through the Brandenberg Gate where the name of the street becomes Strasse des 17. Juni, past the Reichstag, and through the Tiergarten.

"We're coming to Kurfurstendamm," I said. "There's Ka De We."

"You sure know your way around Berlin."

"Right. As long as it's within a few-mile radius of Ka De We."

We reached beautiful Charlottenberg, where Erica had kept her apartment for more than forty years.

"I know she and Ilonka smuggled things out of your grandfather's house," Joel said. "That's one thing. But holding on to them in the heart of Nazi Berlin during the whole war is another. If she could let you know the pressures they were under. Did your mother's girlfriends have someone close, a relative, an acquaintance, who might have reported them if he or she found out what they were doing? A cousin in the party, an uncle in the Gestapo? A neighbor? Where did they hide the stuff all that time? It's a little embarrassing to ask such questions, but try."

I parked on Erica's tree-lined street. She rang us in to her building. We took the old cage-type elevator to her floor where she stood waiting for us by the gate. We exchanged hugs and kisses, but she spoke not a word. I introduced Joel to her. She gave him a tentative smile. He shook her hand. We followed her into her apartment, and when we entered, only then did she speak, and these were the first words out of her mouth:

"You must be told, Ma-ri-an-na, that I am still ashamed to be a German. We Germans will never outlive what we did."

We sat down to a protracted uncomfortable silence. I decided that I had to be the one to jump in.

"All right, then be proud of the kind of German you are. It's not good to hang on to anger forever."

"Why not? I am eighty-six years old, and it hasn't killed me yet. In my case, maybe it sustains me. If anger is what it takes to remember, then beware if we forget. So, what can one say? What more can one know?"

"I want to know," I said, "any little detail about my grandparents from those days. Before everything happened."

She got short with me.

"Before everything happened?" she parroted. "Don't be delicate with me, Ma-ri-an-na. You mean before they took the Wachsners away. Before they murdered millions." Erica's lips were trembling. "If you want to use euphemisms, why not call it 'the Final Solution,' as they did? If we are to talk about these things, do not think hiding behind more genteel words will sweeten the truth."

She went to the kitchen in a huff and came back with tea and cookies.

"I'm sorry," I said. "You're right. I just want to know about my grandparents after Lotte left."

"It was a terrible day. You want to hear this?"

"All of it."

"Bullies sent by Goebbels were out in force, looking for Jews the day your mother sailed. It was a good thing we were there to escort the professor back to Berlin. Even so, we had to sidestep the louts. He had been so esteemed, masterful, always on top of a situation. Now he was frightened and helpless. It broke my heart to see such a man brought down this way. One day, they came to his school and rounded up his students. Then they put him to work in a munitions factory at hard labor. Long hours. Every day. The poorest food and precious little of it. He was exhausted. Paula was put to labor somewhere else. She was so gentle. I could not bear the thought of such a gentle soul treated this way. They were dependent on us for everything, and there was nothing we could do but see that they had enough food and other essentials. We came twice a week to see them. It is a miracle we were never caught. Aryans were forbidden to enter Jewish homes, but we did this for more than three years. How we got away with it, I just don't know."

"Where did you hide all those things?"

"You know how we Germans love our four o'clock coffee and cake. That's when I would go to Ilonka's, and we hid everything in her closet."

"Do you remember the last time you saw my grandparents?"

"It was the fall of 1942. I went there one day and they were gone."

"What about Ursula? Mutti always thought they were in Africa until the end of the war. Jochen just told us they came back in 1941."

Erica poured another tea and took a long sip. "Perhaps they did. I don't know."

"If Ursula came home, she must have gone to see my grandfather. You would have known. Are you saying you didn't talk to Ursula after she came back?"

Erica took her time before she answered.

"We talked."

Now she spoke at great length about many things and would not allow me to interrupt her. She talked about Paula's unbelievable table and what a treat it was when she and her parents came to dinner at the Wachsners. And she said again how Mutti was first in all her classes through school and was the envy of all her schoolmates. She spoke of a confrontation in the street that she had in broad daylight when an elderly man called Mutti a dirty Jew. Erica got into a screaming match with him and was about to get physical when he ran away.

She told us how she accompanied Mutti everywhere, especially at night to her music sessions with Richard Tauber until he left for England, because there was a curfew for Jews unless they were accompanied by Aryans. She went on about how Mutti should not have become a nurse, that it wasn't good enough for her, that Mutti had so much to give the world and would have been someone great, a humanitarian, she was sure of it, had it not been for Hitler.

I never caught all of her German and don't know what else she said. But never once did she mention the name of Ursula. Finally, she said she was exhausted and needed to lie down. When we said goodbye, Joel reached out to shake her hand, but her arms opened wide for him and she hugged him and gave me a wink over his shoulder. Then she hugged me, and, as we left her apartment, she took my hand and held it to her cheek, which was hot to the touch. I think she also knew it was likely to be the last time we would meet.

It was at this time that I decided I wanted my family archive to come home. I will bequeath it to the Holocaust Museum in Berlin.

CHAPTER 16

Heidelberg

WE LEFT BERLIN AS THE EASTER WEEKEND BEGAN, and on our way, we stopped in Leipzig to see the Gewandhaus. From there, we drove southwest past Jena University, where my grandfather had earned his Ph.D., and through the thrillingly gorgeous mountains of Thüringer Wald. All the while, my mind was racing as I tried to fathom what I'd heard from Jochen and Erica.

"My grandfather was still in Berlin in 1941 when the Namgalies came home. Ursula loved him. How could she not have come to see him?"

"You don't know that she didn't," Joel answered.

"If she had, Erica would've told me."

"Don't jump to conclusions."

We reached Heidelberg in the evening. Gisele lived in Hirschberg, a little town on the outskirts of the city. When she heard us drive up, she came out to greet us with a warmth that deepened every moment we spent with her that lovely Easter weekend. She had a fondue waiting, and we sat in her dining room, dominated by a large framed poster of Miles Davis, trying to sort out why we had never met in all the years I'd been visiting Germany. For one thing, she had been teaching school in another part of the country when I first came. It appeared that Bruno and Ursula had borne a family of teachers. We reminisced about Rena and lamented that all of us never had a chance to be together. Rena had often spoken of Gisele and Christel, the twins who had been her friends since childhood. Gisele told me that Rena always talked of me, too, and she knew Rena and Jochen had planned a trip to California. She told me how much her parents truly adored me.

Gisele said that they had been living in the little town near Berlin that Jochen had mentioned, Soldien, "when Bruno came home after the war."

"He came home after the war?" I exclaimed.

"Yes," said Gisele, "when he was released from a Russian prisoner of war camp."

Joel caught my eye. All my life I'd thought that the Namgalieses had returned from Africa when the war ended in 1945. A few days ago, I heard that they came back in 1941. Now I was being told that Bruno did not stay with them in Berlin, but joined the army. I was stunned.

"Regarding your book," Gisele said, "I know you have questions to ask about my parents. So did we always ask. My sister Eva is the oldest and remembers the most. You will meet her tomorrow."

We were exhausted. Gisele showed us to our room and bade us good night.

"Did I get that right?" Joel asked. "Bruno was in the army?"

"That's the first time I ever heard of such a thing," I said, as I passed out for the night, less from exhaustion than from a fractious overload of new information.

We awoke Easter Sunday to the muffled peals of church bells, calling the faithful to service. The weather was perfect for Easter. Gisele laid out a typical German breakfast of different cheeses and *Schinken* (a German meat, similar to prosciutto) and delicious rolls and, in honor of Easter, chocolate Easter rabbits and colored eggs. Gisele's son Florenz joined us for a hearty breakfast. He was a brilliant young student preparing for high school finals. This was the German family at Easter breakfast. Afterward, we all went out to hunt for Easter eggs, hidden all over the backyard, and had a good laugh at Joel, who found not a one of them, although they were right in front of his nose.

Eva arrived, the firstborn of Bruno and Ursula. Now the only one of the siblings I had not met was Christel.

"You must want to see Heidelberg," she said. "We will take you on a walking tour of the city."

Felix, Gisele's oldest son, a student at the University of Freiburg, arrived home for the holiday and joined us all for a walk around the beautiful old city between the Neckar River and the Rock of Heidelberg. Eva told us that the people here think Heidelberg remained unscathed in all its medieval splendor because its many Jewish professors, who had been dismissed from their posts and fled to America before the war, had instructed the Allies not to bomb it.

"We will have dinner at my house tonight and look through pictures to see if we can find any of your mother."

It was a wonderful walk in Heidelberg, and high above the city is a path where we took pictures of all of us together with the city as a backdrop. Way off, there was the university, for centuries one of the most famous seats of culture and centers of learning in the world. I'm still bewildered that all the culture and learning in the world did not prevent the ardent Nazis, who taught and learned pseudoscience, lies, and nonsense in the schools of the Third Reich, from acting out their "savage gene."

A Chagall poster greets you when you enter Eva's house. She made lamb and potatoes for dinner. Her husband, Peter, a quiet and reclusive man, and Joel hit it off right away. After dinner, Peter brought out his impressive collection of rocks and crystals of geological interest, along with fantastic prehistoric and American Indian arrowheads. One is struck by the sophistication of these pieces and has to reflect that it isn't intellect but the onward march of technology that separates modern men from the ancients who made these weapons. I wondered whether they were used to hunt for food or to kill their fellows, as is the nature of the beast through the millennia.

The men talked archaeology and geology while Eva and I went to the living room and looked through Eva's box of pictures. We went over every one of them but found none of Lotte. Ursula had once told me of a scrapbook she'd kept of Mutti's letters, with pictures of them when they were girls. Eva didn't know where it was and said she would look for it, but no one has ever been able to find it.

Joel and Peter joined us just then, and Joel asked him about his own family pictures. Peter reached down in the pile and picked up a snapshot of a baby in the lap of a Wehrmacht officer.

"That is me on the lap of my father. He 'Sieg Heiled' like the best of them." Peter's inflection was accusatory, contemptuous.

"About the book you are writing," Eva said, "Ursula was ill in her last years. We brought her to Heidelberg to take care of her. A few weeks before she died, we knew she did not have much time. With Papa gone, soon we would never know where they really stood during the war. We decided we had to try again to get answers that all of us had asked for since we were children. Every day we asked her, and at the end, as she lay on her deathbed, she told us.

"It might have been 1943 or 1944 when she was given permission by the military to come from Berlin to visit Bruno at his active duty station. It was at Auschwitz. Before her scheduled time at the camp, she went to visit an old girlfriend who lived in the village. While she was in her apartment, the husband took Ursula aside and made sure the doors and windows were shut. And then he whispered, 'Do you know what they're doing in there? They're killing Jews.'"

Ursula said that she went up to the camp and was told to wait in a kind of atrium. She saw slave laborers working with rubber plants. They were not allowed to speak but pointed upward to the smokestacks. Then Bruno arrived. He took her to a commissary where they had lunch. She said he was SS.

Joel told me the color drained out of my face. Surely, Bruno had known what Ursula would see if he let her come there.

"We are still in a state of shock," Eva said. "We have never told Jochen about this."

"Why haven't you?"

"It would upset him, and there was no need to say anything unless we were sure. Christel tried to get to the bottom of it but has run into red tape. She has been unable to get the records."

"Why did you tell me?"

"You need to know of this possibility because of your book."

"Are there any pictures of Bruno in uniform?" Joel asked.

"When I was very little, I remember a picture on the wall of a man in uniform. When the war ended, Russians with shiny boots came to our house. One of them told my mother to take the picture down and burn it, or he would kill her. The man came often and brought us food. I kept asking her about the picture on the wall, but she always said I was imagining things. That is my earliest memory."

Gisele and Eva were not happy to tell me all this. They knew I was as fond of their parents as their parents had been of me. I was moved by their confidence in sharing such a family dilemma. Eva offered us a place to stay for as long as we liked, if we wanted to come back and spend time in Heidelberg. We knew we would.

In the morning, we began our return home, with Joel definitely at the wheel—destination: Stegen Eschbach. We would spend a few days there, then go on to Zurich for our flight back to Los Angeles. He said I'd been sighing every five minutes since the beginning of this awful revelation, even in my sleep. I wasn't aware of it. He asked me whether I wanted to talk about it.

"I would have died long ago," I said, "if it wasn't for them. No kidding. They literally saved my life. I couldn't be mistaken how much they loved my mother and me. I loved them. And my career began with Bruno. I don't get it. Nobody forced Bruno to become a preacher, a guardian of men's souls. He represented God on earth."

"Maybe they forced him to join the army," Joel said.

"There's no excuse. Herbert Bahr stayed in Africa. Why did they come back to Germany and give their strength to Hitler? Why didn't they stay, too?"

"You don't know if they had that choice," Joel replied.

235

Marianne with Clivia (right), 2002.

"But he was SS."

"Just remember one thing. At least they didn't infect their children with that poison."

"I'm glad my mother—and Rena—never lived to hear this."

Jochen had returned to Zagreb and Fabian to London, but Clivia was still in Freiberg, and neither of us would ever miss a chance to see each other. "Did you learn anything for your book in Heidelberg?" she asked.

"You can hear it from me, but your father must hear it from nobody but his sisters."

I told her about her grandmother's visit with her grandfather at Auschwitz. To say she was shocked could not describe her reaction. It was contrary to every value her parents had inculcated in her. I emphasized that it was of the utmost importance to remember that her grandparents did not pass those ideas on to their children and grandchildren. I told her I was having a bad time with this, too, but I needed proof, and I intended to get to the bottom of it.

When we left for Zurich, Clivia told me to take good care of myself.

"After all," she said, "Who is going to look after my children and enjoy them as grandchildren, if not you?"

No sooner had we arrived home in Los Angeles than Jochen called. He had spoken with his sisters.

"I can't imagine," he said. "If he joined the SS, he was required to take a very serious oath to Hitler. It would have been made very clear what was expected of him."

"Why would Ursula have said this, if it wasn't so?" I asked.

"She was delirious at the end," Jochen replied.

I told him that we were pursuing it from our end and would let him know if we were able to obtain more information.

Then a letter came, written in English, from Christel Namgalies, Jochen and Eva and Gisele's sister, the sibling I never met. I paraphrase, and it speaks for itself.

Dear Marianne,

Even though we have not met, Gisele told me of your visit and about you, so I don't feel I am writing this letter to a stranger.

Regarding Auschwitz, my father worked in the camp for prisoners of war. Most of them were murdered. Although I don't know exactly what my father did, I cannot exclude that he had been one of these murderers.

Concerning the facts of your mother's friendship with my mother, it must be very hard for you to receive information like this. My father, the husband of your mother's girlfriend, a man who had been a guest in the house of your grandparents in Berlin, was perhaps deeply involved in the crimes of the Nazis. And the life of your mother, as a Jewish woman, was so deeply attacked andwas made so difficult by all these crimes. Without this history, your life as a daughter of a victim of the Holocaust, and mine as a daughter of a supposed perpetrator, certainly would have been different.

For years, I have been interested in the psychological consequences that these experiences of our parents have on the lives of their children. Although I am not responsible for the activities of my father, I am influenced through his personal energies. These influences of the parents

237

work in most cases in my country and generation in an unconscious way, and I am interested in making them conscious in order to avoid that they will become destructive once more. The children have a lot of similarities because of the legacy of silence. For me, it doesn't seem to be accidental that we come in contact with each other, unfortunately not 'til after the death of Rena.

I wish you strength and courage for your work and the book about our mothers. Perhaps we will meet when you are in Germany once more.

I read Christel's letter and instantly remembered Bruno's sermon that so inspired his congregation and me, all those years ago on my first trip to Germany. "Forgiveness" was the subject, and the thought came to me that perhaps he chose this message most of all because I was in his congregation that Sunday. Because someday, if and when I found out where he had put "his personal energies" during the war, I would remember.

But I was to experience the same frustration that Christel encountered in trying to uncover the truth. It was a snail's pace of cooperation from different departments and agencies on both continents.

And then I remembered Scott Miller and Sarah Ogilvie of the U.S. Holocaust Memorial Museum. Sarah said to leave the problem to her. A few weeks passed, and she called to tell me that at the end of the war, American troops had captured the personnel files of the SS and brought them out of Germany beyond the reach of the Soviets. The records were housed in Maryland. She had gone there personally, and, with the help of an archivist at the National Archives, she looked through all the databases that could possibly contain information about Bruno Namgalies or his family.

"The surname Namgalies is not listed in the SS index. The index held by the archives is 98 percent complete, so there is little chance that anyone in the family was SS. I hope this information proves helpful. If nothing else, you can rule out that Bruno Namgalies and his family members were in the SS."

You can't imagine what a joy it was for me to tell this to the Namgalies clan. The child of a survivor and the children of a perpetrator had anguished together. Now we had a small measure of relief together.

So what can I say of Bruno? SS or not, he was stationed at Auschwitz. The Wehrmacht did their dirty deeds alongside the SS to protect the purity of German blood. Pastor though he was, he had closed his eyes when he lent himself to the blackest deeds in human history. Jochen could only think that his father had succumbed to *Gleichschaltung*, the mass hysteria that overpowers a person's humanity. But mass psychosis or not, those who committed the crimes are responsible for them.

People always ask where God was while all this was going on. I remember what Benny told me, that God shows up in what we do. If He seems absent from our lives, we have only to look to ourselves to know why.

Epilogue

THE MORNING WE LEFT STEGEN ESCHBACH to go home, I went to the little graveyard where Rena is buried and I tended her grave. Thoughts meandered in my mind, that the soldiers of World War II who are buried here had shed their blood for evil. Perhaps there are some who killed Jews and would turn over in their graves if they knew that a Jewish person was standing on the soil above them. At the gravestone of the professor, I wondered again where he had been in his teaching in the 1930s, and what light he had shed on his students. Or, like so many of his colleagues, did he spread the ignorance all about them from his lectern? And at the grave of the nun, I wondered what she had felt in her heart for my people in the time of their agony.

President Ronald Reagan went to Bittberg where SS are buried and stirred the anger of people who said they should not be so honored, that their presence in hallowed ground defiles it. Who belongs where? Burying the good in holy ground is like preaching to the choir. The soul of a Nazi needs God's purging more than anyone else's.

In the end, all I have are Mutti's words of wisdom from when I was a little girl.

"Most people are good," she said. "There are some who are not. But in this world, *Liebchen*, few among us are at all times the one or the other. *Mehr als das gibt uns nicht zu wissen.* More than this we are not given to know."

Printed in the USA
CPSIA information can be obtained
at www.ICGtesting.com
JSHW012015140824
68134JS00025B/2423